Chinese Research Perspectives on Population and Labor, Volume 6

# Chinese Research Perspectives on Population and Labor

*International Series Advisors*

Cai Fang (*Chinese Academy of Social Sciences*)
Kam Wing Chan (*University of Washington*)
William Lavely (*University of Washington*)

VOLUME 6

The titles published in this series are listed at *brill.com/crpo*

# Chinese Research Perspectives on Population and Labor, Volume 6

*New Economy and Innovation in Employment*

*Edited by*

ZHANG Juwei

*Associate Editors*

YANG Weiguo
GAO Wenshu

BRILL

LEIDEN | BOSTON

This book is the result of a co-publication agreement between Social Sciences Academic Press and Koninklijke Brill NV. These articles were selected and translated into English from the original 《中国人口与劳动问题报告No.18》(*Zhongguo renkou yu laodong wenti baogao*) with financial support from the Innovation Project of the Chinese Academy of Social Sciences.

Translated by CHEN Fuyu, Chongqing Jiaotong University, Chongqing, China.

Typeface for the Latin, Greek, and Cyrillic scripts: "Brill". See and download: brill.com/brill-typeface.

ISSN 2212-7518
ISBN 978-90-04-43579-7 (hardback)
ISBN 978-90-04-43580-3 (e-book)

Copyright 2020 by Koninklijke Brill NV, Leiden, The Netherlands.
Koninklijke Brill NV incorporates the imprints Brill, Brill Hes & De Graaf, Brill Nijhoff, Brill Rodopi, Brill Sense, Hotei Publishing, mentis Verlag, Verlag Ferdinand Schöningh and Wilhelm Fink Verlag.
All rights reserved. No part of this publication may be reproduced, translated, stored in a retrieval system, or transmitted in any form or by any means, electronic, mechanical, photocopying, recording or otherwise, without prior written permission from the publisher. Requests for re-use and/or translations must be addressed to Koninklijke Brill NV via brill.com or copyright.com.

This book is printed on acid-free paper and produced in a sustainable manner.

# Contents

Figures and Tables   VII

1  The New Economy: Concepts, Characteristics, and Their Effects on
   China's Growth and Employment   1
   *Zhang Juwei, Zhao Wen, and Wang Boya*

2  Economic Transformation and New Employment   22
   *Xiang Jing*

3  An Analysis of the Changes to Labor Relations under the
   New Economy   44
   *Xie Qianyun*

4  Employment and Work on Online Ride-Hailing Platforms: a Study of Didi
   Platform Data   67
   *Wu Qingjun, Yang Weiguo, Wang Qi, and Chen Xiaofei*

5  The Role of Platform-Based Companies in Creating Employment
   Opportunities for Laid-Off Workers from Overcapacity Industries:
   a Case Study of the Didi Chuxing Platform   105
   *Zhang Chenggang*

6  Policy Support System for Innovative Industries   119
   *Cai Yifei and Wang Boya*

Index   131

# Figures and Tables

## Figures

1.1 Basic statistics of China's high-tech and patent-intensive industries  3
1.2 By-sector weight of China's new economy  4
1.3 Size, composition, and contribution of China's new economy  7
1.4 China's new-economic employment: size, composition, and contribution  12
1.5 Labor productivity and its growth rates under the new economy  14
1.6 Degrees of employment integration and the value added growth of traditional economic sectors (relative to new-economic sectors)  17
2.1 Changes in China's employment rate 1996–2015  24
2.2 The relationship between economic growth and the employment rate  25
2.3 By-industry growth rates of value added in China 1991–2015  28
2.4 By-industry employment growth rates in China 1991–2015  28
2.5 By-sector growth rates of China's urban employment 2011–2015  32
2.6 Regional individual employment boosted by electronic trading  33
2.7 Per capita income boosted by the development of information technology  33
3.1 Weekly working hours of Chinese urban employees (2002–2014)  50
3.2 Dispute settlement rates of labor and personnel dispute arbitration institutions (2005–2015)  56
4.1 Distribution of online ride-hailing drivers by age  70
4.2 Distribution of online ride-hailing drivers by gender  71
4.3 Education levels of online ride-hailing drivers  71
4.4 Household registration status of online ride-hailing drivers  72
4.5 Working conditions of online ride-hailing drivers  73
4.6 Marital status of online ride-hailing drivers  73
4.7 Number of minor children in online ride-hailing drivers' families  74
4.8 Number of household members among online ride-hailing drivers' families  74
4.9 Number of employed household members among online ride-hailing drivers' families  75
4.10 Average monthly individual income of online ride-hailing drivers  75
4.11 Average monthly household income of online ride-hailing drivers  76
4.12 Average monthly household expenditures of online ride-hailing drivers  76
4.13 Number of properties owned by online ride-hailing drivers  77
4.14 Local property value possessed by online ride-hailing drivers  77
4.15 Household bank loans or private borrowings  78

| | | |
|---|---|---|
| 4.16 | Household car loans held by online ride-hailing drivers | 78 |
| 4.17 | Part-time drivers' monthly income from regular jobs | 83 |
| 4.18 | Weekly working days of part-time drivers in regular jobs | 84 |
| 4.19 | Working hours per day of part-time drivers in regular jobs | 84 |
| 4.20 | The five social insurances provided by regular employers | 85 |
| 4.21 | Housing provident fund provided by regular employers | 86 |
| 4.22 | Commercial insurances provided by regular employers | 86 |
| 4.23 | Previous jobs of full-time Didi drivers: working days per week | 90 |
| 4.24 | Jobless period before becoming full-time Didi drivers | 90 |
| 4.25 | Previous jobs of full-time Didi drivers: monthly income | 91 |
| 4.26 | Previous jobs of full-time Didi drivers: working hours | 91 |
| 4.27 | Average monthly ride orders accepted by Didi drivers | 96 |
| 4.28a | Average monthly ride orders accepted by full-time Didi drivers | 96 |
| 4.28b | Average monthly ride orders accepted by part-time Didi drivers | 96 |
| 4.29 | Average monthly driving hours of Didi drivers | 97 |
| 4.30a | Average monthly driving hours of full-time Didi drivers | 97 |
| 4.30b | Average monthly driving hours of part-time Didi drivers | 98 |
| 4.31 | Average monthly income of Didi drivers | 99 |
| 4.32a | Average monthly income of full-time Didi drivers | 99 |
| 4.32b | Average monthly income of part-time Didi drivers | 99 |
| 5.1 | The relationship between provincial GDP growth rate and the proportion of otherwise unemployed Didi drivers | 111 |
| 5.2 | The relationship between the growth rate of provincial per capita GDP and the proportion of Didi drivers from the coal and steel industries | 111 |
| 5.3 | Temporal distribution of Didi registration | 113 |
| 5.4 | Temporal distribution of first ride orders on Didi | 113 |
| 5.5 | Temporal distribution of registration and first transactions on Didi by workers affected by capacity reduction in the steel and coal industries | 115 |

## Tables

| | | |
|---|---|---|
| 1.1 | China's new economy: value added and proportion in GDP | 5 |
| 1.2 | Size of China's new-technology and new-model sectors | 7 |
| 1.3 | China's new-economic employment: size and proportion | 10 |
| 1.4 | Employment in China's new-technology and new-model economic sectors | 11 |
| 1.5 | Integration of traditional sectors with new-economic sectors in 2007 | 15 |
| 1.6 | Integration of traditional sectors with new-economic sectors in 2012 | 16 |
| 2.1 | By-industry employment growth rates in China from the 9th to 12th five-year plan periods (percent) | 27 |

# FIGURES AND TABLES

| | | |
|---|---|---|
| 4.1 | Description of family burdens | 80 |
| 4.2 | Regular jobs of part-time Didi drivers | 81 |
| 4.3 | Social security provided by regular employers | 85 |
| 4.4 | Previous jobs of full-time Didi drivers | 87 |
| 4.5 | Full-time Didi drivers' participation in commercial insurances | 92 |
| 4.6a&b | Full-time Didi drivers' participation in social security | 92–93 |
| 4.7 | Job characteristics of sample Didi drivers | 94 |
| 4.8 | Average monthly ride orders accepted by Didi drivers | 95 |
| 4.9 | Average monthly driving hours of Didi drivers | 97 |
| 4.10 | Average monthly income of Didi drivers | 98 |
| 4.11 | Average monthly income of Didi drivers (by type of city) | 100 |
| 5.1 | Number of workers affected by capacity reduction who found work on the Didi platform in pilot provinces (thousand) | 112 |
| 6.1 | Major supportive documents for the development of innovative industries | 122 |

CHAPTER 1

# The New Economy: Concepts, Characteristics, and Their Effects on China's Growth and Employment

*Zhang Juwei, Zhao Wen, and Wang Boya*

China's new economy covers a wide range of new industries and new business models. It has not only provided a new direction for China's industrial restructuring and upgrading, but also a new sense of momentum for the country's economic growth. Compared with the traditional economic model, the new economy is typified by higher productivity and faster growth. From 2007 to 2016, the new economy achieved an average annual growth of 16.1 percent, 1.9 times as fast as China's GDP growth, and an annual employment growth of 7.2 percent, 22 times as fast as the overall employment growth. Over the same period of time, the number of China's new-model sectors, now a major part of the new economy, grew by an average of 20.6 percent and gained 7.7 percent annual employment growth. By 2016, new-economic sectors accounted for 14.6 percent of China's GDP and 10.1 percent of the overall employment growth. What's more, China's new economy has had a significant effect in terms of boosting the development of related industries. In 2016, new economy-boosted sectors accounted for 8.1 percent of China's GDP in terms of value added and 6.4 percent of the country's overall employment growth.

## 1 China's New Economy: Size and Contribution to Growth and Employment

Following the 2008 global financial crisis, an innovation-driven new economy has emerged that has gradually developed into a major engine for global recovery and economic growth. More importantly, it has given rise to the restructuring of both international trade and the division of labor, which marks a new stage in the innovation-based development of the global economy. As a result, many countries have foregrounded new-economic development as a key strategy in the race to dominate a new round of economic and technological development. For example, at the end of 2009, the Obama administration launched a strategy known as the "Reindustrialization of America," which was intended to establish a new system of high-end industries that would provide sufficient support for American economic growth in the years ahead, to revitalize local industry by returning to the real economy, to promote domestic high-end manufacturing and boost US exports, and to ultimately achieve a sustained and balanced growth on the part of the US economy. Similarly, the European Union set out the Lisbon Strategy in 2000, one of the goals of which was to make EU the most competitive knowledge-based economy in the world by 2010. This was followed by the Europe 2020 strategy, which proposes to invest 3 percent of the EU's GDP in research and development for a knowledge- and innovation-based smart economy.

In China, plans are being made for the further development of its new economy—in particular, its high-tech industries, strategic emerging industries, and intellectual property-intensive industries. In general, the new economy has been growing rapidly in China over the past decade. From 2007 to 2012, the value added of the country's new economy increased by 19.6 percent annually, and from 2012 to 2016, the figure was 12.5 percent. In 2016, the new economy accounted for around 14.6 percent of China's GDP. Meanwhile, China has seen a notable growth in the employment figures of its new-economic sectors over the same decade. From 2007 to 2012, China saw an annual employment growth of 9.2 percent in its new-economic sectors and 4.7 percent in its new-economy-boosted sectors. From 2012 to 2016, however, employment growth slipped down to an annual rate of 4.7 percent its new-economic sectors. Currently, new-economic sectors account for about 10.1 percent of China's overall employment.

## 1.1 China's New Economy: Size, Composition, and Contribution to Growth

While China has not yet released the complete statistics of its new-economic development, we do have access to those of its high-tech and patent-intensive industries. As core parts of the country's new economy, high-tech and patent-intensive industries accounted for 4.8 percent and 12.2 percent, respectively, of China's GDP in 2015 (See Figure 1.1). According to China's *Industrial Classification for National Economic Activities* (Version GB/T 4754-2011), the term "high-tech industries" covers 62 businesses falling within six major sectors: medical manufacturing, aerospace equipment manufacturing, electronic and telecommunication device manufacturing, computer and other office equipment manufacturing, medical devices and equipment manufacturing, and photographic equipment manufacturing. Chinese patent-intensive industries cover an even wider range of businesses falling into 48 specific businesses under eight major sectors, i.e., information infrastructure, software and information technology services, modern transportation equipment, intelligent

# THE NEW ECONOMY

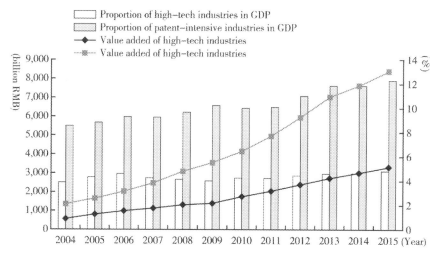

FIGURE 1.1  Basic statistics of China's high-tech and patent-intensive industries
SOURCES: *CHINA STATISTICAL YEARBOOKS; CHINA ECONOMIC CENSUS YEARBOOKS; CHINA STATISTICS YEARBOOKS ON HIGH TECHNOLOGY INDUSTRIES*; AND *CHINA INDUSTRY STATISTICS YEARBOOKS* (SORTED AND RE-CALCULATED BY THE AUTHORS).

manufacturing equipment, bioengineering and pharmaceuticals, advanced functional materials, efficient energy conservation and environmental protection, and resource recycling. In 2016, China's National Bureau of Statistics (NBS) introduced the *Regulations on Special Statistical Reports Concerning New Industries and New Business Models*, which extended the concept of the new economy from high-tech and patent-intensive industries to also cover strategic emerging industries, high-tech business incubation, platform enterprises for crowd-funded operations (crowd investing, crowdsourcing, crowd assistance, and crowd financing), e-commerce businesses (business-to-business e-commerce, e-commerce platforms, and online retail sales), internet finance (online banking), and the development of industrial parks and commercial complexes.

Based on the aforementioned concept of the new economy and current statistics, we have estimated the size, composition, and overall contributions of China's new economy. By "size" and "composition," we refer to the value added and structure of China's new-economic sectors, respectively. And by "contribution," we refer to both the direct contribution (that of new-economic sectors proper) and indirect contribution (that of new-economy-boosted sectors) of China's new economy. Using the Input-Output Table released annually by the NBS, we calculate the size, composition, and both the direct and indirect contributions of China's new economy. We first give weight to each sector in the Input-Output Table to indicate the proportion it makes up of the new economy, and then conduct our calculations based on the input-output relations among the sectors.

We have to weigh the new-economic proportions in each sector because, on the one hand, only certain specific sectors under certain major sectors are categorized as new-economic, and, on the other hand, even though many major sectors are classified as totally new-economic, they have not been singled out in the Input-Output Table. Referencing the NBS *High Technology Industry Classification (Manufacturing)*, *High Technology Industry Classification (Services)*, *Strategic Emerging Industry Classification (2012)*, and *Patent-Intensive Industry Classification (2016)*, we give weight to each specific sector in the Input-Output Table in order to measure how much of each is new-economic, and then calculate the overall value added of those "partially new-economic sectors," as well as the new-economic proportions in them. Figure 1.2 shows the weight of the new economy by sector below.

In 2007, the value added of new-economic sectors amounted to RMB 2,122.2 billion, accounting for 8 percent of China's GDP; that of new-economy-boosted

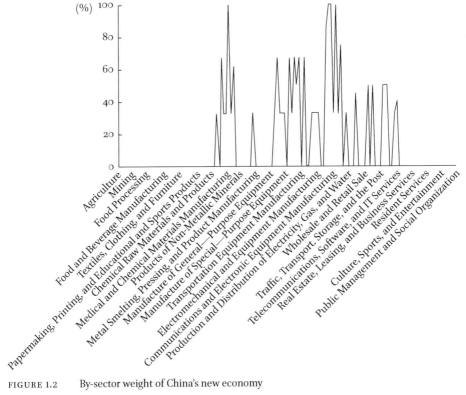

FIGURE 1.2   By-sector weight of China's new economy

# THE NEW ECONOMY

TABLE 1.1    China's new economy: value added and proportion in GDP

| Year | Indicator | Direct contribution | Indirect contribution | Total |
|---|---|---|---|---|
| 2007 | Value added (billion RMB) | 2,122.2 | 1,537.9 | 3,660.2 |
| | Proportion in GDP (percent) | 8.0 | 5.8 | 13.8 |
| 2012 | Value added (billion RMB) | 6,602.7 | 3,926.8 | 10,529.5 |
| | Proportion in GDP (percent) | 12.3 | 7.3 | 19.6 |
| 2016 | Value added (billion RMB) | 10,858.7 | 6,008.8 | 16,867.5 |
| | Proportion in GDP (percent) | 14.6 | 8.1 | 22.7 |

sectors was RMB 1,537.9 billion, accounting for 5.8 percent of China's GDP. This added up to 13.8 percent of China's overall GDP.

In 2012, the value added of new-economic sectors reached RMB 6,602.7 billion, 12.3 percent in China's GDP; that of new-economy-boosted sectors rose to RMB 3,926.8 billion, constituting 7.3 percent in China's GDP. Together, they totaled 19.6 percent of the national GDP. Referring to the development of high-tech and strategic emerging industries in developed countries, we assume that China's new economy will grow 12 percent annually from 2013 to 2016. On an inflation-adjusted basis, in 2016, the value added of new-economic and new-economy-boosted sectors will reach RMB 10,858.7 billion and RMB 6,008.8 billion, respectively, equivalent to 14.6 percent and 8.1 percent (and 22.7 percent in total) of China's GDP.

According to our definition of the term, the new economy can be divided into a "new-technology economy" and "new-model economy." The term "new-technology economy" refers to economic activity for the creation of new technologies and consists of a good many high-tech industries. Over a long period of time, China's new-technology economy has sustained a faster growth than its GDP. From 1996 to 2006, the value added of high-tech industries increased by 20 percent annually and continued to grow by an annual rate of 10 percent from 2007 to 2016. In terms of their weight in China's overall GDP, high-tech industries accounted for 4.3 percent in 2007, 4.6 percent in 2012, and 5.4 percent in 2016. As both the cornerstone and forerunner of the new economy, these rapidly developing high-tech industries have undoubtedly provided powerful momentum for China's new-economic growth.

The "new-model economy" refers to the new-technology-based innovation of production-factor organization to meet the demands for diversified, pluralistic, and personalized products and services, including new links, chains, and models of business operation that are derived from existing industries and sectors. As one of the world's largest economies, China has established a complete industrial system that provides broad space for the cross-modal integration of new-economic sectors. As a result, new economic models are springing up throughout the country, including rural tourism, rural e-commerce, high-tech business incubation, platform enterprises for crowd-funded operations (crowd investing, crowdsourcing, crowd assisting and crowd financing), e-commerce (business-to-business e-commerce, e-commerce platforms, and online retail sales), internet finance, and the development of industrial parks and commercial complexes. In terms of value added, the new-model economy accounted for 3.6 percent of China's GDP in 2007, increasing to 7.6 percent in 2012 and 9.2 percent in 2016.

Taken as a whole, China's new economy has experienced rapid growth over the past decade, increasing by an annual average of 19.6 percent over the period of time from 2007 to 2012 and 12.0 percent from 2012 to 2016. Additionally, new-technology sectors sustained steady growth, up 11.2 percent annually from 2007 to 2012 and 10.9 percent from 2012 to 2016, while new-model sectors experienced even more rapid growth, up 27.5 percent annually from 2007 to 2012 and 12.5 percent from 2012 to 2016.

On the other hand, those sectors that are closely related to and effectively boosted by China's new-economic sectors have also experienced rapid growth over the same period, up by an annual average of 14.9 percent from 2007 to 2012 and by 10 percent from 2012 to 2016.

In terms of proportion to China's new economy, new-technology sectors have been declining while new-model sectors are on the rise over the same period. The former dropped from 55 percent in 2007 to 38 percent in 2012 and 36.5 percent in 2016, while the latter rose from 45 percent in 2007 to 62 percent in 2012 and 63.5 percent in 2016 (See Table 1.2).

The thus encouraging development of the new economy has not only benefitted from favorable conditions in China, but also from the rational direction and strength of relevant policy support.

Above all, it is the country's strong high-tech reserves that prop up the rapid growth of high-tech industries. As opposed to the traditional industrial economy, which is based on traditional industrial technologies, the new economy is primarily grounded on newly introduced high technologies.

Next is the proactive promotion of new economic development by China's policymakers. In 2007, China developed its *11th Five-Year Plan for the Development of High Technology Industries*, indicating the direction its new-economic development would take. In 2010, China issued the *Decision of the State Council*

# THE NEW ECONOMY

TABLE 1.2  Size of China's new-technology and new-model sectors

| Year | Indicator | New-technology sectors | New-model sectors | Total |
|---|---|---|---|---|
| 2007 | Value added (billion RMB) | 1,162.1 | 960.2 | 2,122.3 |
| | Proportion in new economy (percent) | 55 | 45 | 100 |
| 2012 | Value added (billion RMB) | 2,478.4 | 4,124.3 | 6,602.7 |
| | Proportion in new economy (percent) | 38 | 62 | 100 |
| 2016 | Value added (billion RMB) | 3,963.4 | 6,895.3 | 10,858.7 |
| | Proportion in new economy (percent) | 36.5 | 63.5 | 100 |

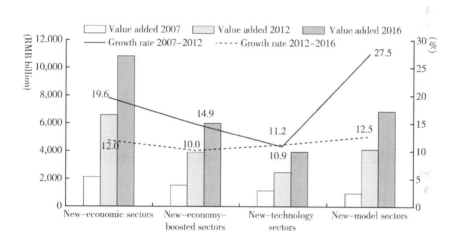

FIGURE 1.3  Size, composition, and contribution of China's new economy
Note: Value added at current prices; growth rates at constant prices.

*on Accelerating the Fostering and Development of Strategic Emerging Industries*, which clarifies the implications of China's strategic emerging industries and underlines key fields of development, such as energy conservation, environmental protections, new-generation information technology, biotechnology, high-end equipment manufacturing, new energy sources, advanced materials, and energy-efficient automobiles. Formulated in 2012, the *12th Five-Year Plan for the Development of Strategic Emerging Industries* determines the goals, key orientations, and major tasks necessary to the development of strategic emerging industries in the 12th Five-Year Plan period. It was soon followed up by the *Guiding Catalogue of Key Products and Services in Strategic Emerging Industries*, which elaborates industrial and product classifications. Developed in 2016, the *13th Five-Year Plan for the Development of Strategic Emerging Industries* further points to strategic emerging industries as the main focus of the new round of technological and industrial changes, as well as being the key to obtaining new growth momentum and new competitive advantages. Therefore, it is essential that we foreground the development of strategic emerging industries to China's overall economic and social development during the country's 13th Five-Year Plan period, while, at the same time, putting all efforts towards a new, modern industrial system, so as to promote sustainable economic and social development.

Finally, China has enormous advantages for its new-economic development, both traditional and unique. It has a huge domestic market supported by the rapidly expanding consumption capacity of the Chinese people; it is rapidly accumulating further human capital, instilling an ever-increasing awareness of innovation and excellence among its people; it has a solid foundation for traditional industrial development and, finally, an irreplaceable manufacturing capacity. Apart from those traditional advantages, China also has unique advantages to its new-economic development. The country's ongoing economic restructuring and adjustment has not only enriched economic forms and consumption demands, but also brought about many opportunities for the development of new-economic sectors. For example, after a long period under a planned economy, the Chinese people have formed a more concrete and in-depth understanding of the old economic system, and are much more capable of having an objective view that posits the new economy as the integration of both market and planned economies. China's economic composition does not only contain advanced employed sectors, but also a large number of traditional, self-employed sectors. Judging by the standards of industrialization, such traditional self-employed sectors are unlikely to avoid being sidelined or even eliminated due to their low levels of standardization. From a new-economic perspective, however, their diversified and differentiated products and services are exactly what people need in the current era.

## 1.2 *Employment Growth under the New Economy: Size and Structure*

Employment is fundamental to people's livelihood. From the very beginning, it has been a matter of public concern as to how many job opportunities the new economy can create. By far there have been quite a number of reports that have analyzed employment growth under the new economy. For example,

THE NEW ECONOMY                                                                     9

Didi Research and CBNData released their *Big-Data Report on Intelligent Mobility 2016*, according to which the Didi Outing ("*Didi Chuxing*") platform provided flexible job opportunities for up to 17.509 million people in 2016, 2.384 million of whom were former employees in China's overcapacity industries and 0.875 million of whom were veterans. The School of Labor and Human Resources at Renmin University of China also concluded its *Research on Employment Growth Boosted by the Alibaba Retail Platform*, saying that the platform had created a total of 30.83 million job opportunities in 2015, 11.76 million of which were transactional positions, 4.18 million of which were supportive positions (including 2.03 million in e-commerce logistics and 2.15 million in e-commerce services), and 14.89 million of which were derivative positions in upstream and downstream Alibaba-boosted sectors, such as manufacturing, wholesale, finance, logistics, and services. Given the above, we still have some questions when we look at the overall picture: most notably, is such employment growth in China's new-economic sectors enough to offset the loss to its traditional sectors?

To answer this question, we have calculated the new-economic employment and new-economy-boosted employment figures using the aforementioned by-sector weight and Input-Output Table. In this context, "new-economic employment" refers to the number of employees in new-economic sectors, which is the new economy's direct contribution to China's overall employment; for its part, the term "new-economy-boosted employment" refers to the increase in the number of employees in those new-economy-boosted sectors that are engaged in the supply of products and services to new-economic sectors, which constitute the new economy's indirect contribution to the overall employment. The calculation itself goes something like the following: suppose there are Sector A and Sector B. If the new economy accounts for 20 percent of Sector A (i.e., 20 percent in weight) and if Sector B invests in Sector A, then 20 percent of Sector B's total input in Sector A is taken to be boosted by the new economy, and the equivalent number of employees (i.e., 20 percent in Sector A's total employment) is taken as the indirect contribution of the new economy to overall employment in Sector A. In order to make the results more accurate and reliable, we have calculated the employees of each sector in the NBS Input-Output Table, which is based on the NBS statistics of both the average wages and total wages of urban sectoral employment and other types of employment. Taking into meticulous consideration all of the above as well as the by-sector weight and the input-output relations, we get the new economy's direct and indirect contributions to employment as well as their respective proportions of overall employment (See Table 1.3).

TABLE 1.3    China's new-economic employment: size and proportion

| Year | Indicator | Direct contribution | Indirect contribution | Total |
|---|---|---|---|---|
| 2007 | Size (million people) | 41.91 | 32.93 | 74.84 |
| | Proportion in overall employment (percent) | 5.4 | 4.3 | 9.7 |
| 2012 | Size (million people) | 65.06 | 41.45 | 106.51 |
| | Proportion in overall employment (percent) | 8.5 | 5.4 | 13.9 |
| 2016 | Size (million people) | 78.19 | 50.01 | 128.20 |
| | Proportion in overall employment (percent) | 10.1 | 6.4 | 16.5 |

As Table 1.3 shows, in 2007, new-economic employment (direct contribution) was 41.91 million people, accounting for 5.4 percent of overall employment; the new-economy-boosted employment (indirect contribution) was 32.93 million people, accounting for 4.3 percent of overall employment. They added up to 9.7 percent of China's overall employment that year.

In 2012, new-economic employment and new-economy-boosted employment amounted to 65.06 million and 41.45 million people, accounting for 8.5 percent and 5.4 percent of overall employment, respectively. They added up to 13.9 percent of overall employment.

By referencing the growth rates of high-tech and strategic emerging industries, we assume that China's new economy grows by 4.7 percent from 2013 to 2016. By our calculations, new-economic employment will reach 78.19 million people in 2016, accounting for 10.1 percent of overall employment; the new-economy-boosted employment will reach 50.01 million people, 6.4 percent of overall employment. These categories will add up to 16.5 percent of China's overall employment.

Specifically, the proportion of new-technology sectors in terms of China's overall employment has increased from 1.1 percent in 2007 to 1.5 percent in |2012 and 1.7 percent in 2016, and that of new-model sectors is up from 4.4 percent in 2007 to 7 percent in 2012 and 8.4 percent in 2016. In terms of the proportion of the new-economic employment, the new-technology sector has slightly decreased over the same period, accounting for 20 percent in 2007,

THE NEW ECONOMY

18 percent in 2012, and 16 percent in 2016; on the contrary, however, the new-model sector has demonstrated a steady increase, from 80 percent in 2007 to 82 percent in 2012 and 84 percent in 2016. It follows that, compared with the new-technology sector, the new-model sector has a greater capacity to boost employment growth.

As can be seen in Figure 1.4 below, China's new-economic sectors gained an annual employment growth rate of 9.2 percent and boasted 4.7 percent annual employment growth in relevant sectors between 2007 and 2012. Over this same period of time, new-technology employment increased by 6.3 percent annually and new-model employment by 9.9 percent annually. With the deceleration of the country's overall economic growth, however, the growth of China's new-economic employment has also slowed to an annual rate of 4.7 percent between 2012 and 2016, and that of new-economy-boosted sectors to 4.8 percent annually. Listed separately, the annual employment growth of new-technology sectors was 2.8 percent and that of new-model sectors was 5.1 percent over this same time period. Nevertheless, these figures are still much higher than China's overall employment growth (by 0.4 percent annually from 2007 to 2012 and 0.3 percent from 2012 to 2016) and even more so compared to that of its traditional sectors (by -0.5 percent annually from 2007 to 2016). Admittedly, new-economic sectors are already a cornerstone of China's employment growth.

TABLE 1.4    Employment in China's new-technology and new-model economic sectors

| Year | Indicator | New-technology sector | New-model sector | Total |
|------|-----------|----------------------|------------------|-------|
| 2007 | Employment (million people) | 8.43 | 33.48 | 41.91 |
| | Proportion in new economy (percent) | 20 | 80 | 100 |
| 2012 | Employment (million people) | 11.44 | 53.62 | 65.06 |
| | Proportion in new economy (percent) | 18 | 82 | 100 |
| 2016 | Employment (million people) | 12.78 | 65.40 | 78.19 |
| | Proportion in new economy (percent) | 16 | 84 | 100 |

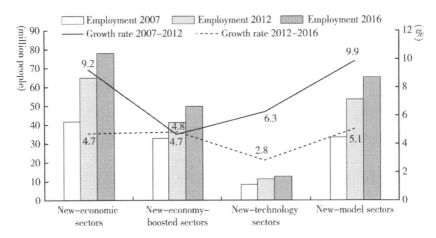

FIGURE 1.4   China's new-economic employment: size, composition, and contribution

## 2   The New Economy as a New Momentum

Although it started relatively late, China's new economy is being rapidly developed. During the 12th Five-Year Plan period, new-economic sectors—in particular energy conservation, new-generation information technology, logistics, biotechnology, high-end equipment manufacturing, new energy, advanced materials, and new-energy automobiles—experienced rapid growth in the country. In 2015, in terms of value added, strategic emerging industries accounted for 8 percent of China's GDP with significant improvements in their capacity for innovation and profitability. In several fields, such as new-generation information technology, biotechnology, and new energy, many Chinese enterprises are already among the most competitive on the international market. Meanwhile, major breakthroughs in China's high-speed rail, communications, space equipment, and nuclear power equipment sectors have also emerged, with a good number of emerging industry clusters—each with an output value of over RMB 100 billion—strongly supporting regional economic transformation and upgrading across the country. On the other hand, the upsurge in mass entrepreneurship and innovation and the extensive integration of emerging industries both facilitate and accelerate the transformation and upgrading of China's traditional industries, and also give rise to numerous new technologies and products, gaining new momentum for the country's economic growth.

## 2.1   *Labor Productivity in the New Economy*

In essence, economic development greatly depends on whether scientific and technological achievements can be converted into material productive forces and whether existing relations of production can adapt to such a conversion. A serious problem with the Chinese economy as it stands now is the imbalance and mismatch between supply and demand. On the one hand, despite inadequate demand overall, a significant portion of China's medium- and high-end consumer demand—with sufficient purchasing power behind it—is not being adequately satisfied on the domestic market. Consequently, many Chinese consumers resort to overseas purchasing agents for higher-end daily necessities. On the other hand, the country's overcapacity industries are still in possession of many resources, resulting in insufficient mobility and use of productive factors, such as human resources, capital, and land. This leaves China's economic development with the short end of the stick, namely, the mismatch between supply and demand, which is due to the lack of an effective domestic supply coupled with a strong demand in certain sectors of the Chinese economy. To solve this problem, it is necessary to, on the one hand, moderately expand the aggregate demand, and on the other hand, strengthen structural reforms on the supply-side in order to improve both the quality and efficiency of the supply system, to cultivate new momentum for development, and to realize the ultimate transformation and upgrading of the Chinese economy.

Why might the new economy boost national industrial transformation and upgrading? The key lies in the fact that the new economy facilitates the conversion of science and technology into productive forces and thus improves overall productivity. Figure 1.5 is a comparison of labor productivity as well as its growth in new economic sectors, new-economic-boosted sectors, new-technology sectors, new-model sectors, and traditional economic sectors. As we see, new economic sectors are significantly higher than traditional economic sectors in terms of the absolute level of labor productivity. For example, the labor productivity of new economic sectors was RMB 101,000, but only RMB 68,000 in traditional economic sectors in 2012. Of all the new economic sectors, new-technology sectors are the highest in terms of labor productivity. For example, the labor productivity was RMB 217,000 in new-technology sectors in 2012, but it was only RMB 77,000 in new-model sectors in the same year. In terms of the growth rate of labor productivity, new-model sectors exhibited the fastest rate of growth over the period of time from 2007 to 2012, followed by new-economic-boosted sectors. Yet from 2012 to 2016, new-technology sectors were the fastest in terms of the growth of labor productivity, followed by new-model sectors. That being said, traditional economic sectors lagged behind

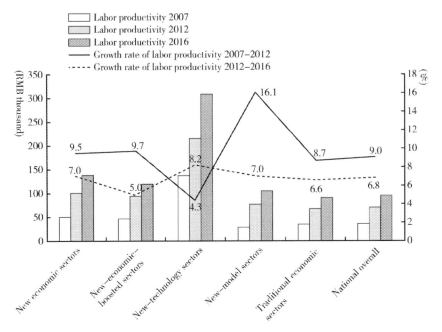

FIGURE 1.5    Labor productivity and its growth rates under the new economy
Note: Labor productivity at current prices; growth rates at constant prices.

new economic sectors over both periods, either in terms of the absolute level or the growth rate of labor productivity. This is exactly the key as to why the new economy can boost industrial transformation and upgrading.

## 2.2    *Sectoral Integration and New Forms of Employment*

China's new economy neither stands alone nor prospers as a unique sector. Rather, it is closely intertwined with other sectors. An important reason why it is able to boost the growth of other economic sectors lies in the new economy's propensity towards sectoral integration. In this context, the function of sectoral integration refers to the new economy's ever-increasing correlation with traditional sectors/industries, which ultimately boosts the development of these other industries/sectors, as well as new-economic sectors. At present, sectoral integration plays a leading role in the development of many of China's industries, particularly in employment among the new-model sectors. Given that China is equipped with a complete range of industries, the new economy can be found almost in every industry and sector of the Chinese economy and, consequently, there is enormous room for China's new economy to initiate sectoral integration and to drive the growth of other sectors. To some degree, new economic sectors play a decisive role in China's national economy. In order

THE NEW ECONOMY                                                                    15

to elaborate on the new economy's role in sectoral integration, we have introduced the concept "employment integration" between new economic sectors
and other sectors of the Chinese economy.

In this case, "employment integration" refers to the proportion of new-
economy-boosted employment in the overall employment of a sector. In
Tables 1.5 and 1.6, we have listed the highest and lowest ten sectors in 2007
and 2012, respectively, in terms of their employment integration within the
new economy. Further, if we withhold the 2007 statistics from the 2012 statistics, we get the changes in the employment integration numbers. By their
very nature, some sectors—mainly public services—are of a low degree of

TABLE 1.5    Integration of traditional sectors with new-economic sectors in 2007

| Highest ten traditional sectors | Integration (percent) |
| --- | --- |
| Electronic component manufacturing | 54.4 |
| Basic chemical raw material manufacturing | 40.5 |
| Electrical cable and equipment manufacturing | 29.1 |
| Air transportation | 25.0 |
| Waste and scrap | 23.8 |
| Steel smelting and rolling processing | 22.2 |
| Non-ferrous metal smelting and rolling processing | 22.1 |
| Non-ferrous metallurgy and alloy manufacturing | 19.2 |
| Other electrical machinery and equipment manufacturing | 19.1 |
| Research and experimental development | 18.3 |

| Lowest ten traditional sectors | Integration (percent) |
| --- | --- |
| Manufacturing of ships and floating devices | 0.02 |
| Fishery | 0.01 |
| Public management and social organization | 0.01 |
| Liquid milk and dairy products | 0.00 |
| Agriculture, forestry, animal husbandry, and fishery services | 0.00 |
| Convenience food manufacturing | 0.00 |
| Machinery manufacturing for agriculture, forestry, husbandry, and fishery | 0.00 |
| Public facility management | 0.00 |
| Social welfare | 0.00 |
| Sports | 0.00 |

employment integration with new-economic sectors, such as education, sports, social welfare, and public management and social organization. In contrast, other sectors—such as storage, electronic component manufacturing, automobile manufacturing, and the production and distribution of gas—have responded rapidly to the opportunity for development brought about by the new economy, and correspondingly increased their employment integration with new-economic sectors.

As we see in Figure 1.6, if we sort all the sectors according to their degrees of employment integration with new-economic sectors and compare the result with the growth rates of their value added, we will find something proportional, that is, the higher the degree of employment integration, the faster a sector grows in terms of value added. For sectors with an employment

TABLE 1.6    Integration of traditional sectors with new-economic sectors in 2012

| Highest ten traditional sectors | Integration (percent) |
| --- | --- |
| Electronic component manufacturing | 98.4 |
| Storage | 73.0 |
| Basic chemical raw material manufacturing | 51.1 |
| Non-ferrous metal smelting and rolling processing | 41.4 |
| Automobile manufacturing | 40.2 |
| Production and distribution of gas | 34.0 |
| Special chemical products, explosives, and fireworks products | 33.4 |
| Pipeline transportation | 29.8 |
| Other electronic devices | 29.5 |
| Rubber products | 23.3 |

| Lowest ten traditional sectors | Integration (percent) |
| --- | --- |
| Education | 0.07 |
| Feed processed products | 0.06 |
| Dairy products | 0.05 |
| Public management and social organization | 0.04 |
| Ships and related installations | 0.01 |
| Fishery | 0.01 |
| Agriculture, forestry, animal husbandry, and fishery services | 0.00 |
| Convenience food manufacturing | 0.00 |
| Social welfare | 0.00 |
| Sports | 0.00 |

# THE NEW ECONOMY

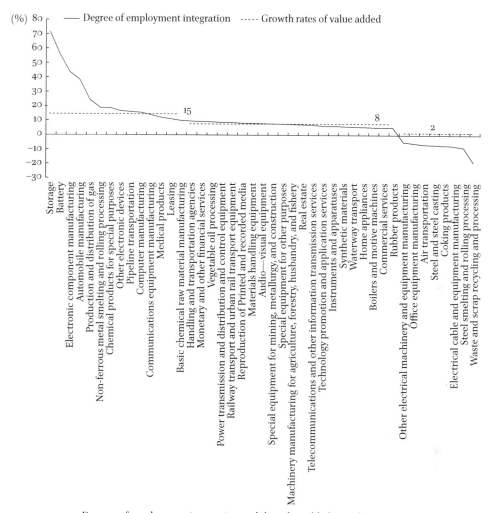

FIGURE 1.6   Degrees of employment integration and the value added growth of traditional economic sectors (relative to new-economic sectors)

Note: Limited by its size, Figure 1.6 has omitted 80 sectors that range between -5 percent and 5 percent in terms of the degree of employment integration.

integration degree of over 10 percent, the growth rate of their value added averages 15 percent. Similarly, for sectors with an employment integration between 5 percent and 10 percent, their value added increases by 8 percent on average. For those sectors with an employment integration below -5 percent, their value added increases only by 2 percent on average. Obviously, under the new economy, sectoral integration—in particular the integration of various forms of employment—has become an important aspect of China's economic growth.

In fact, the degree of employment integration reflects new changes brought about by the new economy to the forms of employment available in China.

When looking ahead to a new round of global industrial revolution as well as a sci-tech revolution, the next five to ten years will be a key period before such revolutions finally emerge. During this period, some labor-intensive industries may shift away from China, but many innovative sectors of the economy will emerge and bring about new job opportunities that will more than make up for the shrinking employment that results. From 2007 to 2012, for example, some sectors rapidly increased their degrees of employment integration, and thus significantly improved their overall employment. As the new economy is running a race against time, great changes are taking place both for China's industrial structure and its employment market.

If we make good use of online platforms and significantly reduce the transaction costs for employment in the emerging new-economic sectors, such as the sharing economy and electronic commerce, we will be able to facilitate rapid docking between the supply side and the demand side, while the new form of employment will weaken the relationship between job-seekers and economic organizations. In this way, we can significantly increase employment flexibility. Such job seekers are usually more open-minded in terms of employment philosophy. They are either starting their own businesses or are working independently as journalists, actors/actresses, network anchors, coaches, beauticians, translators/interpreters, or deliverymen. Some of them may work multiple jobs. For such people, the boundary between employment and self-employment is already blurred. No matter whether they are strong or weak as a group, they all have the chance to earn income in the era of the new economy. Even though job opportunities in the traditional sense appear few and far between, people can still get themselves hired. This fact is at the core of the new form of employment. It is a cross-enterprise organizational economy. Of course, such an unorthodoxly organizational form of employment has broken down the traditional employment relationship between the employee and employer, and is thus at risk of employment security. Accordingly, it was highlighted in the *communiqué* of The Fifth Plenary Session of the 18th CPC Central Committee that China will strengthen support for flexible employment and new forms of employment. Meanwhile, this requires legal consideration to adequately protect those hired in new forms of employment.

## 3 Conclusions and Policy Suggestions

The new economy not only serves as a new impetus for China's economic growth; it also represents a new field for China's employment and a new orientation for China's industrial restructuring, transformation, and upgrading. The new economy is grounded in innovation, and is therefore stronger in terms of innovative momentum. The new economy is better planned than ever before. It values differentiated consumer demands and is therefore able to better coordinate the relationship between production and consumption. The new economy offers a chance to improve the country's economic efficiency and to narrow the gap between economic cycles. Compared with the traditional economy, the new economy is typical of higher productivity and faster growth. From 2007 to 2016, China's new economy increased by an annual average of 16.1 percent, 1.9 times as fast as China's GDP growth; employment in China's new economic sectors increased by 7.2 percent annually, 22 times as fast as the country's overall employment growth. In particular, the new-model sectors grew by 20.6 percent annually and new employment in these sectors increased by 7.7 percent annually over the same period. In 2016, the new economy accounted for 14.6 percent of China's GDP and 10.1 percent of China's overall employment. Meanwhile, the new economy has already had a significant effect on the growth of other industries/sectors. In 2016, new-economy-boosted sectors accounted for 8.1 percent of China's GDP and 6.4 percent of overall employment growth.

As innovation-driven emerging industries gradually develop into the major driving force behind global economic recovery and growth, global economic development can be said to have entered a new era, while the international division of labor and trade patterns continue being restructured. The 13th Five Year-Plan period serves as a decisive stage in the formation of China as a moderately prosperous society in all respects. It is also a period of strategic opportunity for the development of China's new economic sectors. According to the *13th Five-Year Plan for the Development of China's Strategic Emerging Industries*, China's new economic sectors will constantly expand and grow into new factors driving China's economic and social development by the year 2020. Meanwhile, they will give rise to a large number of new, cross-sectoral growth points and boost an annual new employment figure of one million people over the same period.

In order to solve the previously described supply-demand mismatch and imbalance within the Chinese economy, developing the new economy and boosting employment in new economic sectors is key, as is guiding national investment through consumption and supply by demand. The new economy has brought about new models and patterns of both consumption and employment, and is bound to wipe out certain jobs while creating a number of new jobs. In order to adapt to such changes, each individual laborer must acquire new knowledge and skills. Macroscopically speaking, it is important that our social policy effectively support at-risk groups in terms of employment and that, further, our reformation be accelerated to break down all types of barriers against new-job creation and to facilitate the ease with which new economic sectors support China's steady economic growth, structural adjustment, and improvements to worker well-being.

Specifically, in order to boost new employment, we must first give equal weight to both the quantity and structure of domestic employment. With the development of new economic sectors, China's industrial structure is optimizing and its economic output is improving, but this comes with the associated problem of structural unemployment. Accordingly, we must start with the real conditions of different regions, sectors, and groups of people, and focus on the key aspects of employment and the major contradictions therein. We must also implement differentiated policy in accordance with the reality on the ground and make sure that our strength is concentrated on those most in need, so as to preemptively resolve the problem of structural unemployment.

Secondly, we must make efforts on both the supply and demand sides, so as to balance the two on the human resources market. We must stick with the national orientation towards demand, strengthen laborers' capacity to increase the quality of their own work, and facilitate their constant improvement. We must not only conduct the supply-side reform of our human resources market, but also foster a new momentum for economic development. On the one hand, we must expand the development of industries and sectors with strong employment capacities. On the other hand, we must enhance the capability of our economic growth to create even more jobs, and optimize the supply-demand structure of our human resources market.

Thirdly, we must coordinate the roles of the market with those of the government and, in doing so, enhance the capability of our economic development to create jobs. We must fully implement the *13th Five-Year Plan for the Development of China's Strategic Emerging Industries* by vigorously developing new models of both the economy and emerging industries, so as to constantly expand new fields of employment. At the same time, we must promote new products and the application and demonstration of new services, accelerate the industrialization of those new products and services, and steadily allow them to absorb employment opportunities. We must speed up the development of various forms of the new economy, facilitate the establishment and development of more micro- and small-sized economic entities than have previously been allowed, develop new models of employment, and provide fertile, future-oriented, and cross-sectoral soil for employment and entrepreneurship.

We must also improve the existing mechanisms for innovation and creation and increase our domestic capacities for economic upgrading and the expansion of employment opportunities.

Fourthly, in order to encourage innovation, we must be inclusive and prudent in terms of formulating regulatory rules for emerging industries. We must actively innovate and experiment with new regulatory approaches for emerging industries, so as to create a more relaxed environment for their development. We must also develop China's developmental guidelines for the sharing economy and boost the healthy development of the country's sharing economy by improving related policies—such as the protection of consumers' rights and optimizing the environment for sharing economy development—and by relaxing control over market entry, innovating regulatory approaches, and guiding the multi-party management of sharing economy development. On the other hand, we must also support the development of new forms of employment, e.g., new types of self-employment, by improving our institutions regarding employment and labor security, etc.

Finally, we must deepen our reformation of the statistical administrative institutions and improve our statistical services insofar as concerns emerging industries. On the one hand, we must intensify our reformation and innovation of China's statistical system. On the other hand, we must carry out comprehensive, systematic, and in-depth statistical surveys of China's new economic sectors/industries, such as high-tech industries, strategic emerging industries, high-tech services, internet finance, science and technology business incubators, crowd investing enterprises, crowd financing platforms, urban complexes, development zones, etc., and promptly release the survey results to the public.

CHAPTER 2

# Economic Transformation and New Employment

*Xiang Jing*

In 2015, China's tertiary industry accounted for over 50 percent of the country's national GDP even while experiencing significant internal structural adjustments. With the increased reform of China's economic institutions and mechanisms, the development of a creative and innovative economy is in the process of accelerating the replacement and/or upgrading of traditional sectors/industries by emerging sectors/industries. Driven by the development of the new economy, creation- and innovation-related jobs are on the rise. Yet during this process, China is faced with certain adjustments in terms of its employment growth. On the one hand, China's working-age population is declining, and the growth rate of China's employment is simultaneously slowing down. Industrial transformation and upgrading—while strengthening the tertiary industry's capacity to absorb the labor force—has widened regional gaps in economic development and employment growth. On the other hand, digital technology has not only accelerated industrial integration, but has also made higher demands on the quality of laborers' skills. A new round of employment growth is emerging in tandem with the disappearance of many traditional jobs. This is almost inevitable in the course of China's transformation and upgrading. In view of the above factors, we hereby advise relevant departments at the state level to increase the collection of individual employment statistics in addition to the statistics of employment in larger institutions and units. It will be conducive to further study the development of China's new employment in light of the effects new business models and industrial integration have on employment figures, and this report will provide more detailed information for China's social and economic development.

## 1 China's Employment in a New Stage of Development

Since 1991, China's employment rate has been on the decline. Yet at present, this decline has already narrowed, and the employment rate has stabilized. If we compare the relationship between the stages of economic development and the country's employment rates, we can conclude that China will be faced with major adjustments in its employment growth. On the one hand, during the 12th Five-Year Plan period, the country's tertiary industries have surpassed its secondary industries in terms of their proportion in China's overall GDP. Meanwhile, China's tertiary industry has entered a stage characterized by upgrading and improvement, and therefore is now an important field for absorbing employment. On the other hand, inside China's tertiary industries, information- and digital-technology-based sectors are more capable of absorbing employment. Yet in the new round of employment growth, new forms of employment—in particular, platform-based companies—are increasing significantly and serve as sources of important momentum for regional economic growth in China.

## 1.1 *Constant but Narrowing Decline in the Employment Rate versus Adjustments to Employment Growth*

From the 9th Five-Year Plan period to the 12th Five-Year Plan period, the variation in China's overall employment rate may be roughly divided into three stages. The first stage (1996–1999) is marked by a high employment rate. During the 9th Five-Year Plan period, China's employment rate slipped from 76.54 percent in 1996 to 76.08 percent in 1999, down by 0.46 percentage points, but the overall employment rate remained at a high level (76.08 percent) at the end of 1999. The second stage (2000–2010) was characterized by a rapid decline in China's employment rate, from 73.76 percent in 2000 to 68.05 percent in 2010. From the 10th Five-Year Plan period to the 11th Five-Year period, China's employment rate dropped by 5.72 percentage points, a drop which averaged a decline of 2.86 percentage points in each of the five-year plan periods. The third stage (from 2011 onward) has witnessed a slowdown in the decline of China's employment rate, which has stabilized between 67 percent and 68 percent. During the 12th Five-Year period, China's employment rate only dropped from 67.89 percent to 67.50 percent, down by 0.39 percentage points. Currently, the continuous decline in China's employment rate is coming to an end, but it remains extremely difficult for China to increase its employment rate against the aging of its population.

During the 13th Five-Year Plan period—and over the medium and long term—China is very likely to agonize over its employment transformation.

In the first place, it is rather difficult for China to sustain the current employment rate at around 68 percent. This has been demonstrated by the widening gap between China's labor participation rate and its employment rate. From the 9th Five-Year Plan period to the 11th Five-Year Plan period, China's employment rate was about one percentage point lower than its labor participation rate. Between 2010 and 2015, however, this gap widened to 1.92 to 2.3 percentage points and continues to widen further. Following the in-depth adjustment

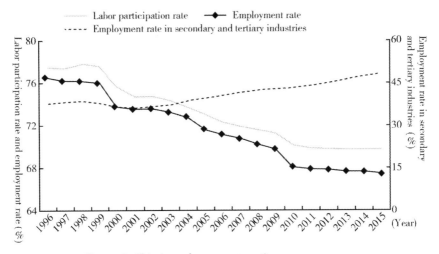

FIGURE 2.1    Changes in China's employment rate 1996–2015
Notes:
1. Labor participation rate = Economically active population/Working-age population over 15;
2. Employment rate = Employed population/Working-age population over 15;
3. Employment rate in secondary and tertiary industries = Employed population in secondary and tertiary industries/Working-age population over 15.
SOURCE: *CHINA STATISTICAL YEARBOOK 2016*.

of China's demographic structure, which is a result of the country's implementation of its family planning policy, China's working-age population will have to face the aging problem in the future. What's worse, many of China's working-age population who are still at the prime of their life (in their forties or fifties) are relatively low in terms of human capital and lack the necessary foundation to learn new skills and adapt to new science and technology. Consequently, they will probably fail to adapt themselves to a new round of scientific and technological revolutions aimed at boosting China's economic development. Therefore, China faces a big challenge in sustaining the current employment rate.

Secondly, historically speaking, China is faced with the challenge of whether or not its employment will step into a new round of growth. For humankind, every technical innovation has brought about scientific and technological progress, a more convenient life, and a significantly higher level of social welfare. Yet every technological revolution has also resulted in the disappearance of some traditional industries and employment sectors. In fact, using time-series data or global cross-section data, we can easily find a reversed U-shaped relationship between the employment rate and the level of economic development.

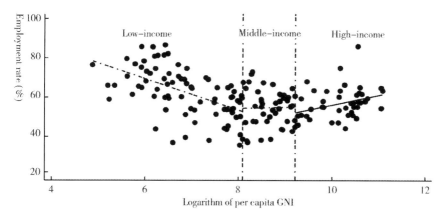

FIGURE 2.2  The relationship between economic growth and the employment rate
Notes:
1. Based on the 2010 statistics of per capita GNI and employment rates of 176 economies. Specifically, "income" refers here to per capita net income in inflation-adjusted dollar terms, and "employment rate" equals the employed population divided by the total population (International Labor Organization).
2. According to the World Bank's 2010 thresholds, low income is per capita GNI below USD 3,233.5; middle income is per capita GNI between USD 3,233.5 and USD 9,982.7; and high income is per capita GNI above USD 9,982.7.
3. Through calculations, the income elasticity of employment ($R^2$) is:
(Low income) ln(Employment)=5−0.13* ln(perGNI), $R^2$=0.2766 which is significant in 99 percent of the confidence interval;
(Middle income) ln(Employment)=3.67+0.037*ln(perGNI), $R^2$=0.0051 which is insignificant; and
(High income) ln(Employment)=3.14+0.088*ln(perGNI), $R^2$=0.1159 which is significant in 95 percent of the confidence interval.
SOURCE: THE WORLD BANK, *WORLD DEVELOPMENT INDICATORS*, (2016).

According to some estimates, in the low-income stage, the income elasticity of employment is negative, i.e., every percentage point growth in the national income equals a 0.13-percentage-point decline in the employment rate; in the middle-income stage, the income elasticity of employment is 0.037 percent but statistically insignificant; and in the high-income stage, the income elasticity of employment is positive (around 0.088 percent). If China succeeds in both crossing the middle-income trap and sustaining a 5 percent annual growth of its GDP, it will be able to increase its employment rate by 0.44 percent annually. Using the 2016 projected figure of China's total employment, this translates into 3.41 million new jobs (or newly employed people). In view of recent changes in China's demographic structure, especially the one-million-person decline of the country's working-age population (15–64 years old) between 2015 and 2016, the new round of economic growth is bound to increase the demand for the country's labor force, indicating a positive trend for China's overall employment in the future.

Finally, in the future, another challenge for China's employment market will be how to improve labor productivity in order to address the growing demand for a new-type industrial workforce that results from China's economic transformation.

### 1.2 Accelerated Upgrading of China's Tertiary Industry: a New Point of Employment Growth

From the 9th Five-Year Plan period to the 12th Five-Year Plan period, China experienced a significant decline in the growth of its economically active population. During the 9th Five-Year Plan period, China's economically active population grew by 6.06 percent annually, but the figure dropped to 1.92 percent during the 12th Five-Year Plan period. According to some predictions, China's economically active population will decline further but tend toward stability during the 13th Five-Year Plan period. Synchronizing such a decline, the growth of China's employment will slow down, too, during the 13th Five-Year Plan period, while overall employment tends to also be stable over the same period. It should be noted that significant changes are taking place to the industrial structure of China's employment, and, in particular, that China's tertiary industry is accelerating its upgrading and has grown into an important field for the new round of employment growth taking place in China.

Since 2012, the tertiary industry has outweighed the secondary industry in terms of China's GDP and has been growing more rapidly than the other industries in terms of value added. According to statistics, the primary, secondary, and tertiary industries accounted for 9.42 percent, 45.27 percent, and 45.31 percent, respectively, of China's GDP in 2012. In 2015, the figures were 8.88 percent, 40.93 percent, and 50.19 percent, respectively. In terms of the growth rate of value added, the primary industry dropped from 4.5 percent in 2012 to 3.9 percent in 2015; the secondary industry dropped from 8.4 percent in 2012 to 6.1 percent in 2015; but the tertiary industry sustained its growth rate at around 8 percent.

In the course of China's industrial restructuring, changes are also taking place within each industry's capacity to absorb employment. Take the tertiary industry for example. During the 10th and 11th Five-Year Plan periods, the tertiary industry's capacity for employment absorption was weakened. Currently, however, China's tertiary industry is undergoing a new round of employment growth. According to statistics, the secondary industry was the largest in terms of China's GDP prior to the 12th Five-Year Plan period. Specifically, employment in China's secondary industry grew by 0.1 percent annually during the 9th Five-Year Plan period; the figure was 15.6 percent annually during the 11th Five-Year Plan period. Meanwhile, the proportion of the tertiary industry in terms of China's overall GDP was on the rise during this same period, but its capacity to absorb employment was significantly weakened, with the annual growth rate of employment slipping from 16.24 percent during the 10th Five-Year Plan period to 9.07 percent during the 11th Five-Year Plan period. During the 12th Five-Year Plan period, it became obvious that the tertiary industry had become the key to China's GDP growth and that, meanwhile, its capacity to absorb employment had also improved significantly. From 2011 to 2015, employment in China's tertiary industry increased by an annual rate of 20.37 percent, eleven percentage points higher than the figure during the 11th Five-Year Plan period.

In terms of the growth rate of employment, the tertiary industry was been the strongest in the years from 1991 to 2015, except for the period from 2004 to 2012, when China accelerated its industrialization, which significantly increased employment in the secondary industry. It was not until 2012 that the tertiary industry surpassed the secondary industry in terms of its proportion in China's GDP. That is to say, from 1991 to 2010, employment in China's tertiary industry was mainly concentrated in lower-end services, and the tertiary industry was far behind the secondary industry in terms of output value per head.

TABLE 2.1    By-industry employment growth rates in China from the 9th to 12th five-year plan periods (percent)

| Period | | Economically active population | Overall employment | Primary industry | Secondary industry | Tertiary industry |
|---|---|---|---|---|---|---|
| 9th Five-Year Plan | 1996–2000 | 6.06 | 4.55 | 3.51 | 0.10 | 10.58 |
| 10th Five-Year Plan | 2001–2005 | 3.03 | 2.54 | −8.12 | 9.44 | 16.24 |
| 11th Five-Year Plan | 2006–2010 | 2.72 | 1.50 | −12.55 | 15.60 | 9.07 |
| 12th Five-Year Plan | 2011–2015 | 1.92 | 1.35 | −17.58 | 0.66 | 20.37 |

SOURCE: *CHINA STATISTICAL YEARBOOK 2016.*

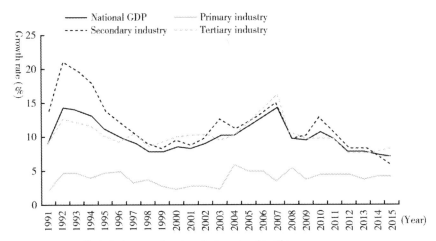

FIGURE 2.3   By-industry growth rates of value added in China 1991–2015
SOURCE: *CHINA STATISTICAL YEARBOOK 2016*.

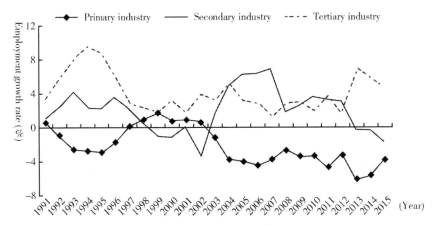

FIGURE 2.4   By-industry employment growth rates in China 1991–2015
SOURCE: *CHINA STATISTICAL YEARBOOK 2016*.

Since 2012, however, the gap between the tertiary and secondary industries in terms of output of labor narrowed significantly. Currently, during this 13th Five-Year Plan period, China's tertiary industry has entered a critical stage of upgrading and transformation and is becoming increasingly capable of absorbing employment—in particular in the higher-end services.

ECONOMIC TRANSFORMATION AND NEW EMPLOYMENT          29

## 2    New Employment: Characteristics and Development

During the 13th Five-Year Plan period, the digital economy and the sharing economy have been rapidly developing in China, providing great opportunities for both innovation and entrepreneurship. In the process, information and digital technologies are being widely used, and industrial integration has been greatly enhanced. Under such circumstances, many people have pointed out that the development of China's new economic sectors and new models of business will give birth to new employment, and that it is therefore necessary to redefine employment.[1] By itself, however, it is unnecessary to re-define the term "employment" (an activity to which a laborer devotes time in return for a payment or remuneration), no matter how technologies develop and how integrated industries become. In our view, the new employment is "new" simply because it is quite different from traditional employment only in the ways and modes of payment/return received by the laborer engaged in an economic activity.

### 2.1    *Characteristics of New Employment*

Compared with traditional employment, new employment is characterized by higher flexibility, higher personal value of laborers, new labor relations, and new demands on laborers' skills.

### 2.1.1    Flexibility

Nowadays, the new economy has greatly enhanced laborers' job flexibility, both in terms of working modes or working hours. In fact, the advent of the internet and digital technologies in China has given rise to a large number of cooperative "platforms" such as bicycle-sharing platforms, JD.com, Taobao, Didi Chuxing (Didi Outing), and more. As a result, many people in possession of certain resources (e.g., private cars, production lines, etc.) or competent personnel are able to make money simply by making use of such platforms. Be they full-time or part-time drivers on Didi Chuxing or sellers on Taobao or WeChat, these self-employed individuals have invariably found a job by taking advantage of the various internet platforms. What's more, the application of digital technology has sped up the development of every link—from production to communication and circulation—and has naturally broken the

---

1  Hao Jianbin 郝建彬, "Shuzi jingji jiuye zai dingyi yu xin jiuye si da guandian 数字经济'就业再定义'与新就业4大观点 [Re-Defining Employment in Digital Economy and Four Views on New Employment]," http://www.aliresearch.com/blog/article/detail/id/21353.html.

traditional, fixed work schedule, so that these laborers are able to flexibly arrange their working hours.

### 2.1.2 Laborers' Personal Values

The new generation of laborers has grown up with the widespread availability of the internet and with significant contact with digital technology. They are used to communications and acquisitions that use digital and information technology. In the future, for most job seekers on China's labor market, employment will be aimed more at self-actualization than for making a living. For example, 71 percent of graduates in the year 2016 expressed their wish to achieve their own, self-guided career when they were looking for a job. That is why those born in the 1990s prefer an open, free, and relaxed enterprise culture.[2] In particular, those born in the second half of the 1990s prefer to work in emerging industries closely related to the digital economy, in positions such as anchors, online celebrities, and so on. Under the rapid development of the new economy, the internet-based economy, and the digital economy, job seekers are challenging the traditional values of ranks, levels, and long-term employment, and more and more new recruits are beginning to express their concern over self-actualization.

### 2.1.3 "Platform + Individual"

In the future, the online-platform-based type of employment and the traditional mode of employment will develop concurrently for a not-inconsiderable period of time, during which process they will also integrate with and promote each other. In fact, with the rise of the Internet of Things (IoT), many laborers in China have begun seeking various "odd jobs" on third-party sharing platforms. At the same time, following the rise and application of new technologies, traditional organizations are establishing more flexible job markets. Those doing "odd jobs" are usually quite proficient and skilled. In order to adapt to market demands, both sides organize temporary service platforms according to market conditions. In this new mode, the relation between laborers and platforms is no longer the traditional individual-organization type of employment. It is more of a coalition and cooperative, whereby both sides receive their payment by relying on their skills or resources. Such a new type of relation is a deviation from the rigid personnel relationship found within traditional organizations,

---

2  Zhaopin 智联招聘, "Erlingyiliu chunji jiulinghou zhichang xiaoxiang diaocha 2016 年春季90后职场肖像调查 [The Spring 2016 Survey on the Employment of the Post-1990s Generation]; Erlingyiliu nian yingjie biyesheng jiuye diaocha [Survey on the Employment of 2016 Graduates]."

but at the same time it is also a challenge to related laws and regulations in practice, e.g., *The Labor Contract Law of the People's Republic of China.*

### 2.1.4    Laborers' Skills

Scientific and technological revolution has not only brought profound changes to industries and business models, it has also raised new requirements for laborers. At present, digital and information technology is integrated into every industry and sector, so much so that the application of such technology has become a necessity for almost every position. Just as computers have begun to enter every office, this is a very basic requirement in the information and data era. Meanwhile, driven by the above-mentioned technical progress, minimum job requirements are increasing as well. For example, traditional ways of marketing are being replaced by digital modes of marketing; traditional business-information analysis is being converted into big-data analysis; and traditional media operators are turning into operators of a mixed-modal entertainment industry. This means higher requirements for the skills and comprehensive quality of job seekers on the market. Therefore, in order to realize a new round of economic growth and take full advantage of the technological revolution, it is necessary to constantly train our laborers.

### 2.2    *The Development of New Employment in China*

Due to the lack of official statistics on China's new employment, we must base our analysis on the NBS statistics of those sectors that are closely related to digital and information technologies. Generally speaking, China's new employment—which is grounded in the growth of data technology—is developing rather quickly, but it varies significantly from region to region.

Currently, the tertiary industry is the major field experiencing employment growth in China. In particular, data-technology-based sectors—such as information transmission and software—are the strongest in terms of their capacity to absorb employment. According to available statistics, employment across China's urban work units increased from 144.133 million in 2011 to 180.625 million in 2105, up by 5.06 percent annually. Specifically, employment in information transmission, software, and information technology services increased from 2.128 million in 2011 to 3.499 million in 2105, up by 12.89 percent annually. Over the same period, employment in leasing and business services, scientific research and technical services, and wholesale and retail sales—all of which are closely related to the internet economy—grew by an annual rate of 13.08 percent, 7.51 percent, and 7.28 percent, respectively. What's more, with the increase in electronic commerce and online shopping platforms, China's urban employment in traffic, transportation, storage, and the post

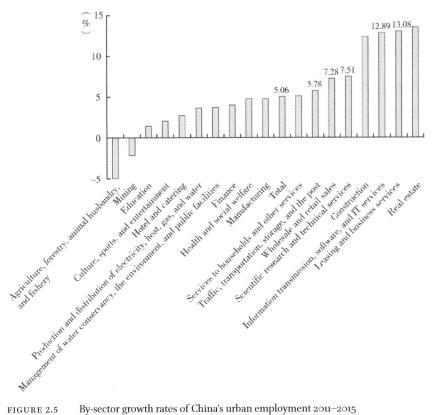

FIGURE 2.5   By-sector growth rates of China's urban employment 2011–2015
SOURCE: *CHINA STATISTICAL YEARBOOK 2016*.

increased by 5.78 percent annually from 2011 to 2015, higher than the national average level.

While the application of digital and information technologies promotes the rapid development of China's new employment, it also provides more flexible job opportunities for individuals. Against the background of deepening labor-market reforms in China, individual businesses are becoming increasingly active. In particular, there is a significant increase in the new employment figures predicated on e-commerce platforms. The wider the application of digital and information technologies in a region, the faster the economy and employment numbers grow. We can observe the proportions of electronic trading in the overall enterprise business activity of China's provincial-level divisions in 2015 and compare them with the growth rates of individual employment in the same year. We then conclude from the observation that the more frequently electronic trading takes place in a province, the faster the province's individual employment grows. The correlation between electronic trading and individual employment is 0.9 and statistically significant at 95 percent.

ECONOMIC TRANSFORMATION AND NEW EMPLOYMENT

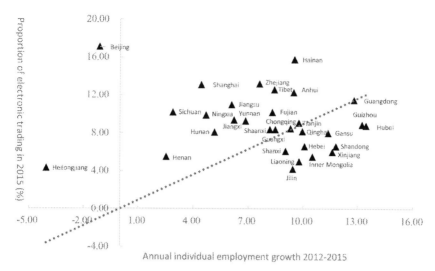

FIGURE 2.6   Regional individual employment boosted by electronic trading
SOURCE: *CHINA STATISTICAL YEARBOOK 2016*.

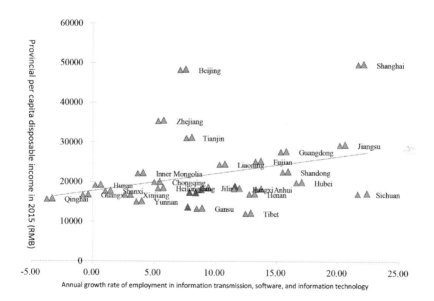

FIGURE 2.7   Per capita income boosted by the development of information technology
SOURCE: *CHINA STATISTICAL YEARBOOK 2016*.

The rapid development of the data economy has not only increased the demand for information and communications workers, but has also boosted regional employment and widened already-existing regional gaps. According to our calculations, a 1 percent growth in the employment figures of China's IT industry equals an increase of RMB 434.8 in per capita disposable income for corresponding provincial-level divisions. At present, the development of information technology is extremely uneven in China, with the eastern coastal region having five to eight times the size of the IT industry found in China's central and western regions. In 2015, 0.68 million, 0.254 million, 0.283 million, and 0.353 million laborers were working in information transmission, software, and information technology in Beijing, Shanghai, Jiangsu, and Guangdong, respectively. By contrast, the figures in Yunnan, Guizhou, and Sichuan collectively numbered less than 90,000, while Qinghai, Ningxia, and Xinjiang together totaled only 45,000.

## 3       Challenges for the Development of China's New Employment

While the world shifts from a reliance on internet technology toward digital technology, the digital economy has become an effective force for boosting the rapid development of the Chinese economy. The wide application of digital technology has brought about a sharing economy of RMB 3,945 billion,[3] and has provided women and disabled workers with the means to better enter the labor market. The application of digital technology across various industries, however, is changing conventional models of business and traditional ways of thinking, and is also having a comprehensive and profound influence on China's employment. On the one hand, the digital economy is creating job opportunities and changing the employment structure in brand-new ways. On the other hand, it has deepened already existing inequalities within the job market. The new round of technical revolution has widened the gap between manual and mental workers, between skilled and unskilled workers, and between single- and multiple-disciplinary talents. Such new conditions have imposed new requirements on the government.

First, the shift towards digital technology has deepened existing inequalities in the labor market. It is therefore an urgent task to stabilize the labor market

---

3  According to statistics from China E-Commerce Research Center, China's Sharing Economy totaled RMB 3,945 in size, up by 76.4 percent; some 60 million people provided sharing-economy services, up by 10 million people over 2015; and 5.85 million people shared the economic platforms, up by 0.85 million people over 2015.

and adapt China's labor structure to market development. For example, those in their 40s and 50s are still a major part of China's labor market, and they will not retire for another ten to twenty years. This group of laborers, however, is vulnerable in terms of their human capital accumulation, especially when tested by the rapid development of technology, which also proves the cruelty of market-based competition. According to statistics, employees aged between 25 and 39 accounted for 35.6 percent of all those employed in 2014, while those aged between 40 and 54 accounted for 37 percent. Yet compared with younger workers, the middle-aged possess lower levels of human capital and are more likely to lose ground during the restructuring and transformation of the labor market. In fact, college (and higher) diploma holders accounted for 13.6 percent, 9.7 percent, and 8.5 percent of all laborers aged 40–44, 45–49, and 50–54, respectively. For these laborers, there will be another ten to twenty years before they can retire. For the time being, they must provide for their parents and children. Losing their jobs will add to overall social instability.

Meanwhile, the labor market has significantly increased its demand for inter-disciplinary talents, necessitating the improvement of the education system and further integration between education and skills training in preparation for a future talent contest. The country's new employment has emerged alongside the transformation of its traditional industries, and its demand on employees mainly includes the application of new technology and an understanding and operation of new business and industrial models for development. That is to say, new jobs and new positions require that employees should not only be capable of using digital technology, but also be familiar with the business procedures and patterns of a sector that relies on it. As such, while the current education system has its advantages in terms of teaching basic theory and knowledge, there are obvious deficiencies in the links between campuses and the labor market. Accordingly, we must improve existing training mechanisms to facilitate the updating of some basic knowledge and strengthen the application of knowledge and technology. On the one hand, the government is hereby encouraged to support the establishment of a more efficient training system cutting taxes or subsidiaries and to lowering the cost of new employee training by enterprises. On the other hand, it is necessary to improve the evaluation system of talents on the labor market, to boost the orderly mobilization of talents, to guarantee laborers' interest in further training, and to increase enterprises' input in staff training.

Second, the rise of the platform economy is a challenge to the traditional employment relationship. It indicates that flexible employment is likely to be more common in the future. Yet balancing and protecting the interests of emerging platforms while also limiting temporary employment poses a difficulty. At the same time, under new models of employment and new labor relationships, the effectiveness of the social security system presents yet another challenge for the Chinese government.

Having grown up in the internet era, the new generation of laborers highly values qualities such as personality and independence. On the other hand, the rapid development of the digital economy has caused the conversion taking place on employment relations to shift from a focus on "organization and employee" to "platform and individual". More and more young people choose to freelance by linking themselves with online platforms, relying on their skills, resources, products, or services to make a living. According to the *Report on the Current Situation of Freelancers in China in 2015*, 70 percent of freelancers in China are young people under thirty. The report also predicts that the proportion of freelancers will reach 43 percent by 2020.[4] On the other hand, many institutions initially put into place to protect laborers, such as the minimum-wage system, social security, and other employee benefits stipulated in China's contract law, have not yet been extended to platform-based freelancers—a situation that is likely to give rise to a new type of potential labor-capital disputes. For example, in the UK, Uber drivers accuse the company of treating them like independent contract workers, rather than as normal employees, which has deprived them of normal employees' benefits, such as paid holidays, pensions partially paid by the company, etc. As part of the sharing economy, many drivers and workers for China's Didi and Mobike services are program-based contract workers, instead of formal employees. Such a form of flexible employment has enhanced society's capacity to absorb laborers, but the uncertainty in their labor relationship has caused a non-negligible loss of social welfare on the part of such laborers.

According to the current policy in China, base payment for freelancers' social insurance must fall somewhere between 60 percent and 300 percent of the average monthly wage level of all workers. Yet the income of freelancers varies significantly, while their average salary remains quite low. If their social insurance is paid by themselves alone, many medium- and low-income freelancers will be unwilling to take part in it. In light of such a social insurance design, it is right that the more one pays, the more one enjoys. Yet if we keep in mind that China is a socialist country, we must conclude that the goal of social insurance must aim at improving overall participation as well as the overall level of social security in line with social and economic development. Accordingly, it is necessary to supplement the existing social security system in order to correspond to new types of labor relations on the market, to fully

---

4  "Erling erling nian ziyou zhiyezhe renshu jiang zhanbi 43 percent 2020 年自由职业者人数将占 43 percent [Freelancers to Account for 43 percent in 2020]," *Beijing Evening News* (March 23, 2017).

reflect the nature of Chinas as a socialist country, and to strengthen Chinese citizens' sense of gains from the country's social development.

Third, aspects of the economy for which data are collected for statistical purposes do not adequately reflect market development, and must be unified and standardized. Meanwhile, previous statistical bulletins have not been updated to include information on new employment, despite there being an urgent need for official, authoritative statistics in this regard. First of all, as a concept, new employment rises alongside the new economy and new industry, so when there is no clear definition of either the new economy or new industry, many studies and analyses will necessarily differ in terms of statistical scope. Many media and research centers (e.g., the Boston Consulting Group, Aliresearch, and Zhaopin) have released reports on the development of internet-related industries and e-commerce. When it comes to the application of digital technology, a good variety of new terms—such as the digital economy, the sharing economy, and E-GDP—have emerged. They are all based on digital technology, but there is a world of difference between them. For example, E-GDP is an expenditure approach that calculates all activity related to digital creation, production, services, and application. In other words, E-GDP refers to that part of the value added in all industries of conventional GDP that involve digital technology. In contrast, the sharing economy is a business model[5] instead of an industry, and therefore its accounting usually pays more attention to issues of scale and market value, rather than the value added of an industry, as more befits E-GDP. Comparatively speaking, the digital economy is closer to E-GDP in that it not only has relatively independent economic forms, but that, more importantly, it is feasible to make accounts based on existing industrial classification standards.[6] Until this point, however, no official statistics regarding China's digital economy have been released. Even though many platform enterprises or consultation companies have published information on the size and trends in the development of China's digital economy, such reports are usually based on the market value and size of platform enterprises, rather than their industrial value added. This has led to a fair bit of difficulty in predicting the development of China's digital economy in the future.

Secondly, many industry names in research reports on the nation's media are not consistent insofar as how they adhere to the standards of China's industrial classification for national economic activities, leading to a degree

---

5 Marcus Felson and Joe L. Spaeth, "Community Structure and Collaborative Consumption: A Routine Activity Approach," *American Behavioral Scientist* 21 (1978): 614–624.

6 Kang Tiexiang 康铁祥, "Shuzi jingji jiqi hesuan yanjiu 数字经济及其核算研究 [Digital Economy and Its Accounting]," *Statistics and Decision* 5 (2008):19–21.

of inaccuracy in the citation of such reports. For example, over the past two years, the Internet/E-commerce ranked first in a labor-market application report released by Zhaopin and the China Institute for Employment Research, Renmin University of China. Yet in China's industrial classification for national economic activities, the closest classification is Internet and Relevant Services (Code 64), which is further divided into three sectors: Internet Access and Relevant Services, Internet Information Services, and Other Internet Services. Is Internet/E-commerce included in Internet and Relevant Services (Code 64) in China's industrial classification? Or does it overlap with the latter? So far, there are no clear indicators as to where it might best fit. This has not only caused great differences in research results using different statistical scopes, but has also limited the quotability of such research results when assessing the development of China's emerging industries.

Finally, current job classifications do not adequately reflect the market's demand for technology. A profession has to develop and update alongside the concurrent progress of an industry and/or sector, during which process it keeps changing both its content and the form its activities take. Digital technology has, for its part, accelerated the evolution of jobs in China. A typical example of this is the number of on-site staff. In 2016, the number of on-site staff declined by 14,000 in the Industrial and Commercial Bank of China, but that did not result in a significant decline in the overall number of bank employees. In fact, of these 14,000 people, some 3,000 have shifted to emerging businesses and the other 11,000 have become customer managers.[7] With technological innovation and the improvement of automation and intelligence, many less-skilled positions are being gradually replaced by machines. Meanwhile, the demand for interpersonal communications is increasing. This is not capable of being replaced by machines, and should therefore be the focus for future employment and profession. There may not be much change in the content of such a profession, but it does require higher and more advanced skills. Yet current professional analyses can hardly reflect the changes being brought about by technological revolutions to relevant professions, and have thus caused difficulty in analyzing and predicting the trends of employment.

---

7  Dong Ximiao 董希淼, "Zhongguo yinhangye fengkuangdi chejigou chaiyuan? Shuju jieshi qizhong zhenxiang 中国银行业疯狂地撤机构裁员？数据揭示其中真相 [Chinese Banks Busy Cutting Institutions and Laying off Workers? Statistics Tell The Truth]," *Economic View*, April 10, 2017.

## 4 Conclusions and Policy Suggestions

Historically, the effect of every technical revolution has been to either strengthen or weaken industrial employment. At present, the Chinese economy is at the critical stage in terms of accelerating its transformation in order to overcome the middle-income trap. Meanwhile, China's employment market has entered a new stage of development by following the country's industrial progress. This process, marked by a new generation of digital technology, has allowed the digital economy to boom and has had (and is having) a profound influence on the labor market in China. So, even as traditional jobs continue to disappear, the rise of AI and machines means that the competition between humans and machines is increasingly intense. However, in such a critical period of economic restructuring, it is extremely important to recognize both the positive and negative effects of technical progress on the labor market.

Based on data technology, the new economy is developing rapidly in China's internet, cloud computing, big data, internet of things, and AI sectors. It creates an enormous sense of momentum for China's economic activities and also strengthens China's capacity for innovation and entrepreneurship. In order to develop the new economy and create new jobs, we must promote increased employment in digital-based sectors, such as new retail, pan-entertainment, new finance, new manufacturing, etc. We must also endeavor to improve laborers' skills in digital-technology application, so as to avoid the panic-inducing phenomenon known as "technological unemployment." Additionally, we must improve the correlation between supervision and technology, and establish an open, clean, safe, and reliable employment climate. What's more, we must improve China's social security system and tax system so as to strengthen our capacity for social welfare. Finally, we must optimize the classification and structure of professions, enhance technical-grade division and identification, and better match the labor market's supply and demand.

A. We must focus on the basic services necessary for data technology and boost the rapid growth of employment. Data technology may be limited in terms of directly boosting employment, but the indirect support it provides for employment is substantial. According to estimates by BCG, China's internet sector created some 1.7 million job opportunities in 2014.[8] If we extend the term "employment" to cover the entire new economy, we see that job opportunities increase many-fold. In fact, e-commerce platforms not only drive derivative employment across platform enterprises, sellers, platform management, and

---

8  Boston Consulting Group (BCG), *Year 2035: 400 Million Job Opportunities in the Digital Age*, January 2017.

support services, but also magnify market demand through the use of convenient digital payment. Thus, they indirectly stimulate employment at both the upper and lower streams of the industrial chain in certain fields. Take the retail e-commerce platform Alibaba, for example. It has created 30.83 million job opportunities, such as Taobao shop owners, deliverymen, e-commerce service providers, and many more at both the upper and lower stream of the industrial chain. What's more, the transformation of traditional manufacturing through data technology also creates new job opportunities. As BCG has predicted, the application of machines to auxiliary production and unmanned logistics tools will cause the disappearance of 0.61 million positions by 2020, particularly among those involving assembling, packaging, and production. Meanwhile, there will be 0.96 million new job opportunities in information and data technology services for manufacturing. Therefore, there is going to be a net increase of 0.35 million job opportunities.[9] In view of the in-depth integration of data technology with an increasing number of sectors and fields in the future, it is necessary to focus on data technology and basic services and thereby stimulate the rapid growth of new employment in China's retail sales, entertainment and culture, finance, and manufacturing.

B. We must strengthen education and training related to the application of data technology so as to cope with the risk of increasing structural unemployment that is inherent to industrial transformation and upgrading. Data technology may either strengthen or weaken overall employment. As some research points out, 55 percent to 77 percent of China's current positions will be replaced by intelligent machines, simply because they are considered low-skill positions.[10] Nonetheless, the stimulus on employment effected by data technology is still likely to be a benefit rather than a weakness. This is because AI is still unable to replace human labor in certain fields, such as interpersonal communication, innovation, etc. For example, the rise of e-commerce platforms has resulted in the shuttering of many traditional retail stores, but the demand for retail workers is significantly increasing. The focus of new retail is not on product display as with traditional shops, but on consumer experience and individualized service. Traditional sales evolve into digital sales; business intelligence analysis turns into big-data analysis; the disappearance of many positions on the assembly line is more than made up for by new job opportunities in IT, hardware, data science, engineering, and human-computer interaction fields. That

---

9 Boston Consulting Group (BCG), *Man and Machine in Industry 4.0: How Will Technology Change the Structure of Industrial Labor Force Through 2025?* May 2016.

10 Boston Consulting Group (BCG), *Year 2035: 400 Million Job Opportunities in the Digital Age*, January 2017.

is to say, the rapid development of the new economy will stimulate the demand for inter-disciplinary talents that are not only already familiar with a given industry and business but are also masters of data technology application. Such versatile talents have enormous room for career development and will prove to be the key battlefield in a new "war over talents." As such, we must enhance data technology education from the very beginning, increasing the proportion of computation, science, and engineering offered at every stage of education. We must promote further cooperation between schools and enterprises in order to provide training courses and prepare for the talents that will be needed in the new economy. Meanwhile, we must retrain those laborers already in the labor market and improve the ability of these laborers to apply data technology, so as to avoid the aforementioned panic over "technological unemployment."

C. We must establish a digital society and digital credit management system while also improving market supervision and regulations. Data technology has not only altered the form of many industries but has also changed processes of employment. While job-seekers have individualized demands that require open positions to prove their value, this poses a challenge to the traditional employment relationship. With the in-depth integration of China's new sharing culture, mobile payments, cloud computing, and Location Based Service (LBS) technology, many freelancers and entrepreneurship teams are already on the market that possess the skills, means of production, or final products being sought by employers. They may access any platform at any time and maximize their revenue given their "on-demand" services. As opposed to traditional forms of employment and management, the relationship between a platform and an individual or team is predicated on contracted cooperation, which relies on individual contribution and resources as well as the platform's support for services. This method of organization has been integrated with and has made good use of socialized resources, but it is potentially significantly vulnerable to employment fraud. At the same time, the vast sea of personal information collected by various platforms and online intermediaries has also posed a challenge for social governance. We must therefore establish a digital society and digital credit management system, reinforce the connection between law enforcement and technology, and improve labor market supervision and regulation under the new economy.

D. We must improve China's social security system and system of taxation so as to strengthen our capacity for social welfare. The appearance of platform-based companies has increased the flexibility of jobs, but it has simultaneously put forward new requirements on the government's social governance. Brought up in the internet era, "digital natives" regularly use information technology to communicate and interact with each other, but exhibit little loyalty to their organizations and occupations. Research shows that over 70 percent of freelancers in China were born after 1985.[11] For such freelancers, accounting and the payment of taxes and insurance are more complicated because of their flexible models of employment. Given such circumstances, we must give full consideration to different models of employment, reform our tax system, and establish a big-data income registry and information collection system. We must also take into account the difference in household structure and employment models and improve our individual income tax reporting system in line with that accounting. Meanwhile, we must establish an information exchange mechanism between the collection of taxes and social security and set up a social security system for freelancers under the principle of "tax determines insurance." We must increase our social security coverage and reinforce our existing social security.

E. We must optimize the classification and structure of the professions, enhance technical-grade divisions, and improve the degree of matching between supply and demand on the labor market. The latest *Dictionary of Professions of the People's Republic of China (Revised Edition)* has variously increased or decreased some professions on minor and specific terms, but has not revised the eight major classifications of professions. It has inherited the work analysis approach previously used when classifying professions, without directly reflecting or adjusting the weight of laborers' technology. For example, the new professions of "manicurists" and "e-commerce engineers" both fall into the category of Business and Services Personnel, but are also labeled as Other Business and Services Personnel on minor terms. Yet if we compare the specific work and prospects of the two professions, the latter requires more professional skills, and the demand for such talents will significantly increase over the course of time and as industries continue to upgrade. Following the new round of data technology, many positions are becoming increasingly technical, a typical characteristic of which is the replacement of manual labor by intelligence and the corresponding upgrading of employment structures. We must adapt to the influence of technology on the labor market. We must reflect the technical level of an occupation when we are classifying it. We may refer to the Standard Occupational Classification System of the United States in establishing our own occupational database according to our own classification needs and following an analysis of various jobs. We must follow the regularity of industrial development and heighten the technical requirements imposed on occupational classification. This is not only conducive to increasing

---

11    LinkedIn, *Report on the Current Situation of Freelancers in China in 2015*, 2015.

the correlation between a profession and the market, but also to measuring the skill level of and the demand for human capital within the national labor market.

## Author Biography

Xiang Jing has a Ph.D. and research assistant at the CASS Institute of Population and Labor Economics. Her academic interests include agricultural economics, population shifts, and population structure and economic development.

## References

Boston Consulting Group (BCG), *Man and Machine in Industry 4.0: How Will Technology Change the Structure of Industrial Labor Force Through 2025?* May 2016.

Boston Consulting Group (BCG), *Restructuring Employment in the Internet Age: Three Aspects of the Internet's Influence on Employment in China*, August 2015.

Boston Consulting Group (BCG), *Year 2035: 400 Million Job Opportunities in the Digital Age*, January 2017.

Boston Consulting Group (BCG), *Year 2035: Overcoming the War for Talent Under the Digital Economy*, January 2017.

Felson, Marcus and Joe L. Spaeth, "Community Structure and Collaborative Consumption: A Routine Activity Approach," *American Behavioral Scientist* 21 (1978): 614–624.

Jiang Xiaojuan 江小娟, "Gaodu liangtong shehui zhong de ziyuan chongzu yu fuwuye zzengzhang 高度联通社会中的资源重组与服务业增长 [The Reorganization of Resources and the Growth of Services in a Highly Connected Society]," *Economic Research Journal* 3 (2017): 4–17.

Kang Tiexiang 康铁祥, "Shuzi jingji jiqi hesuan yanjiu 数字经济及其核算研究 [The Digital Economy and Its Accounting]," *Statistics and Decision* 5 (2008): 19–21.

The World Bank, *World Development Report 2016: Digital Dividends*, doi: 10.1596/978-1-4648-0671-1, 2016.

CHAPTER 3

# An Analysis of the Changes to Labor Relations under the New Economy

*Xie Qianyun*

In recent years, China has entered a "new normal" state of economic development, with new conditions for and profound changes to its economic structure. It is within this context that the state has implemented a new employment prioritization strategy. This proactive policy has resulted in greater employment stability in China. Amid such stability and improvements, employment in China has exhibited several new trends, new characteristics, and new patterns.[1] With the Chinese economy entering the aforementioned "new normal," accelerating the development of the new economy and boosting the rapid growth of new technologies, new industries, and new models of business has become an important component of China's supply-side reform, aimed as it is at further and better economic development. Under the new economy, we see new characteristics in the country's industrial structure, the supply and demand of the workforce, and employment conditions and modes. The overall employment conditions have a direct impact on laborers' work and labor relations. Therefore, laborers' work and labor relations are also subject to change under the new economy.

In this chapter, we will begin by analyzing the development of China's new economy and changes in China's employment structure. Based on an analysis of laborers' working conditions and labor relations under the new economy, we will then put forward some suggestions on new developments for work and labor relations under the new economy.

---

1  Zhang Juwei 张车伟, "Shibada yilai woguo jiuye xin tedian he jiuye youxian zhanlüe xin neihan 十八大以来我国就业新特点和就业优先战略新内涵 [New Characteristics of China's Employment Since the 18th CPC National Congress and New Connotations of the Employment Priority Strategy]," *People's Daily*, July 19, 2017.

© KONINKLIJKE BRILL NV, LEIDEN, 2020 | DOI:10.1163/9789004435803_004

## 1 The New Economy and the Development of China's Employment

The new economy refers to that part of the economy that has been boosted by the IT revolution and is led by high-tech industries in the context of economic globalization. It is an economy primarily composed of "Internet Plus," advanced manufacturing, new energy, new material, new models of business, etc.[2] In a way, the new economy integrates several new technologies with the new-technology economy. It represents the direction of economic development in China and demands further development in the future. It reflects high technical levels and advanced business models. It has gained a new sense of momentum for the sustainable growth of the Chinese economy and the steady growth of China's employment figures.

According to the existing development and experience provided by the US and other developed countries, the new economy is generally based on the rapid growth of high-tech industries, such as information and communications. These high-tech industries then help restructure or integrate traditional industries, which are then gradually developed into new industries or transformed into new industries through innovation. Under the new economy, an important characteristic of industrial structural change is the rapid development of services, in particular those related to high- and new technology, such as scientific research and technical services, information transmission, computer services, and software. We can thus predict that, under the new economy, similar changes will affect China's industrial structure in the future, and that the development of the new economy will further promote the adjustment of China's industrial structure and boost the upgrading of China's industrial structure by means of industrial reorganization, industrial integration, and industrial innovation.

Such changes to the country's industrial structure will certainly have an influence on employment and, thus, also have an impact on labor relations. In this chapter, we will briefly analyze possible changes to China's employment structure under the new economy. After that, we will analyze changes in work and labor relations in China. The following are possible new changes in China's employment structure under the new economy.

---

2  Xiang Xiaomei 向晓梅, "Shiying xin changtai fazhan xin jingji 适应新常态发展新经济 [Adapt to the New Normal and Develop the New Economy]," *Economic Daily*, May 5, 2016.

### 1.1 The Capacity of the Tertiary Industry as a Major Field to Further Absorb Employment

While the three major industries undergo structural transformation and upgrading, changes are also taking place to their employment structure, a typical example of which is the rapid increase in the proportion taken up by the tertiary industry. From 2012 to 2016, the proportion of the tertiary industry to overall employment increased from 36.1 percent to 43.5 percent, making it the largest industry in terms of absorbing employment; over the same time period, the proportions of the primary and secondary industries in overall employment decreased from 33.6 percent and 27.7 percent to 30.3 percent and 28.8 percent, respectively.[3] If the current trend of development persists, the tertiary industry will absorb an increasingly large share of laborers. Moreover, under the new economy, the service industry—in particular those service sectors closely related to high and new technology—will develop more rapidly, which will increase employment in China's services.

### 1.2 The Emergence of New Forms of Employment

With the implementation of the Innovation-Driven Development Strategy by the CPC Central Committee and the State Council of China, new industries and new models of business are developing quickly and new forms of employment are emerging, including new fields of employment, new technological means, new patterns of organization, and new concepts outlining employment.[4] New employment takes many specific new forms, including labor-intensive positions on internet-based e-commerce and sharing-economy platforms, or online-platform-based or offline resource marketization, such as food deliverymen for internet-based delivery platforms, logistics couriers for e-commerce platforms, and other labor-oriented but internet-adjacent positions. More importantly, these new industries and new models of business have a significant effect on the employment absorption of various types of laborers. According to statistics provided by China's State Information Center (SIC), over 0.6 billion people took part in the sharing economy in 2016, of which some 5.85 million worked on sharing-economy platforms, up by 0.85 million from 2015.

---

3  NBS. Improvements in Employment and Highlights in People's Livelihood: Fruits of China's Economic and Social Development Since the 18th CPC National Congress, No. 11. http://www.stats.gov.cn/tjsj/sjjd/201707/t20170721_1515384.html.

4  Zhang Chenggang 张成刚, "Jiuye fazhan de weilai qushi xin jiuye xingtai de gainian ji yingxiang fenxi 就业发展的未来趋势，新就业形态的概念及影响分析 [The Future Trend of Employment Development and the Concept and Influence of New Employment]," *Human Resource Development of China* 19 (2016).

## 1.3 *Growth of Small Enterprises*

The rapid growth of small enterprises has created numerous job opportunities, and small enterprises have therefore become one of the main choices for Chinese laborers. Based on experiences seen in developed countries, during the development of the new economy, China's small enterprises—especially emerging high-tech ones—will grow rapidly and absorb many people in the labor market. For example, the new economic period in the US was an era of clustered innovation during which large numbers of high-tech enterprises— both small- and medium-sized—came into being and rose to prominence.[5] These enterprises absorbed large numbers of laborers and created numerous job opportunities. In recent years, employment in large enterprises has decreased, and employment in small enterprises—especially those engaged in services and key industries—is already growing faster than in large- and medium-sized enterprises.[6] We can therefore presume that, with the development of the new economy and new employment, there will also be a large number of small, high-tech enterprises that are based on new science, new technology, and new industries, and that such small enterprises will become one of the major choices for laborers seeking employment opportunities.

## 1.4 *Growth of Informal and Flexible Employment in China*

As the government revises the country's employment policies and adopts various measures aimed at boosting the employment of laid-off workers and people with difficulties finding jobs, there has been visible growth in the employment of such groups of workers, but they mainly tend to choose informal and flexible employment. Meanwhile, informal and flexible employment has also been the choice of many migrant workers. In 2016, there were a total of 273.95 million peasants and 168.21 million migrant workers in China.[7] Based on the current data and trends in development, migrant workers will still remain numerous under the aegis of the new economy, and they will continue to be one of the major forces for informal and flexible employment on China's labor market. Moreover, the further development of high technology and various institutional innovations will encourage professional and skillful technical personnel to find jobs as freelancers.

---

5 Liu Shusheng and Li Shi 刘树成、李实, "Dui meiguo xin jingji de kaocha yu yanjiu 对美国"新经济"的考察与研究 [Observation and Studies on the New Economy in the US]," *Economic Research Journal* 8 (2000): 3–11, 55–79.

6 Guo Tongxin 郭同欣, "Gaige chuanxin chujin le woguo jiuye chixu kuoda 改革创新促进了我国就业持续扩大 [Reform and Innovation Boost China's Sustained Employment Growth]," *People's Daily*, March 29, 2017.

7 NBS. *Report on Monitoring and Survey of China's Migrant Workers 2016* (2016).

## 2 Changes in Laborers' Work under the New Economy

Since the country's reform and opening up, the Chinese economy has been developing rapidly. In this process, Chinese laborers' working conditions have reflected several specific characteristics. For example, working hours are generally getting shorter, but putting in overtime remains a significant phenomenon. This developmental trend resembles prior international experiences, but there are notable differences between China's experience and those seen elsewhere. There are various forms of employment, including formal and informal employment. Working conditions and the environment are improving, and working efficiency is also increasing alongside the development of science and technology, as well as improvements to the quality of laborers themselves. Under the new economy, changes will take place to the country's industrial and employment structures. Some positions will be replaced, and some may gradually change their focus. In this chapter, we will focus on the working hours—including the working hour arrangement and the length of the workday—and working modes common to Chinese laborers, and analyze the changes to Chinese laborers' work taking place under the new economy.

### 2.1 *Changes in Working Hour Arrangements*

Currently, the mainstream working hour arrangement in China is the eight-hour workday that requires laborers to begin and end their workday at a fixed time, such as the nine-to-five pattern. Many employers require their employees to punch the clock to ensure such working hours. Laborers' working hour arrangement is, on the one hand, the result of mandatory provisions on the part of laws, regulations, and their employers. On the other hand, it reflects laborers' decision making in terms of working and leisure hours.

With the further development of the new economy and the emergence of new forms of employment, as well as more flexible working hours in enterprises as they attempt to adapt to market demand, laborers' working-hour arrangements will be more flexible, liberal, and fragmented in the future.

To address the first of these issues, laborers' working-hour arrangements will be more flexible. In order to improve work efficiency and reduce unnecessary working hours, some enterprises have gradually implemented irregular working hours, shift work schedules, night shifts, and other flexible work schedules. For laborers in informal, flexible, and new forms of employment, work no longer occurs between fixed hours—they are entitled to deciding their working hours, work tasks, and even work agenda. Such flexible schedules include the following forms: laborers' completely free arrangement without any fixed working hours; basically fixed working hours with certain flexible free time built in; laborers' free arrangement according to working contents and workplace, and other patterns of flexibility.

Secondly, laborers' working-hour arrangements will become more liberal. Under the new economy and new forms of employment, laborers will be free to decide their own working hours, and in most cases, their working-hour arrangement will be based on the specific conditions of their tasks. When everyone spends his/her time reasonably, it will not only improve their own work efficiency, but also bring more convenience to the lives and work of others. Particularly among some platform enterprises as they are organized under the sharing economy, staff members are both owners of the platform's resources and users of the platform. As long as they finish their designated tasks, such as the completion of a certain number of sales or the creation of profits at a lower cost, etc., then laborers have the right to freely and flexibly arrange their own working hours.

Thirdly, laborers' working-hour arrangements will be more fragmented. Under the new economy, fragmented working hours are the inevitable result of a more flexible and liberal working arrangement. That is to say, laborers' working-hours are no longer a cohesive whole but fragmented according to their work contents and tasks. This is particularly true for those laborers who choose to work for a couple of hours or even just a certain span of seconds. It should be noted that the fragmentation of working hours does not mean breaking down the working hours from a whole into fragments, which makes one extremely busy but inefficient. Rather, it means a more rational arrangement of the tasks by making use of flexible working time. In this model, different tasks are sorted and finished separately, but the working hours remain whole in order to ensure that laborers work efficiently and stay focused.

## 2.2    *Changes in the Length of Working Time*

According to relevant laws and regulations,[8] there are generally two standards outlining Chinese laborers' working hours, namely, there are a standard number of working hours (40 hours per week) and a maximum limit on working

---

8    Article 36 of *The Labour Law of the People's Republic of China* stipulates: "The State shall practice a working hour system wherein laborers shall work for no more than eight hours a day and no more than 44 hours a week on the average." Article 3 of *The Rules of the State Council on Working Hours of Workers and Staff Members* stipulates: "Laborers shall work for eight hours a day and 40 hours a week."

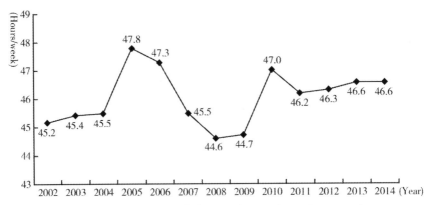

FIGURE 3.1    Weekly working hours of Chinese urban employees (2002–2014)
SOURCE: *CHINA LABOR STATISTICAL YEARBOOKS* 2006–2015.

hours per week (44 hours).[9] However, despite the standard number of working hours and working time arrangement being explicitly stipulated, Chinese laborers in general work too long, and laborers across different industries vary in terms of their actual hours worked.

From 2002 to 2014, urban employees worked 46.1 hours per week on average, longer than the legal maximum of 44 hours per week (See Figure 3.1). During this time, however, there were also three important changes in urban employees' working hours. In 2005, urban employees' working hours peaked at 47.8 hours per week. In 2008, urban employees' working hours fell to the lowest point recorded, coming in at 44.6 hours per week. From 2008 to 2010, urban employees' working hours rose again to 47 hours per week. Yet the figure started to decline slightly starting in 2010, but since then there has been no significant change to it. Therefore, generally speaking, despite the fact that Chinese laborers' working hours have been shortening, they still exceed the legal limits on working hours (40 hours per week), which indicates a serious phenomenon of working overtime.

Working hours vary significantly by sector across the primary, secondary, and tertiary industries, where working overtime is most common in the secondary and tertiary industries. From 2011 to 2014, the fewest number of weekly hours worked were among urban employees in the primary industry (37.4 hours per week in 2014); working hours in all sectors of the secondary industry, however, exceeded the legal limits (40 hours per week)—in mining,

---

9    Lai Desheng, Meng Dahu, Wang Qi 赖德胜、孟大虎、王琦, "Woguo laodongzhe gongzuo shijian tezheng yu zhengce xuanze 我国劳动者工作时间特征与政策选择 [Characteristics of Chinese Laborers' Working Hours and Policy Choices]," *China Labour* 2 (2015):36–40.

manufacturing, and construction, specifically, the average number of working hours even exceeded 44 hours per week; in most sectors of the tertiary industry, overtime averaged around four hours, such that the overall working hours are only a bit too long. In other words, working overtime is quite common among service sectors. In particular, employees in hoteling and catering had to work 51.5 hours per week, which was the longest time logged among all sectors.[10] The working hours of most urban employees were too long, too, and a large proportion of urban employees worked over 40 hours. To some degree, many urban employees have had to accept working overtime as a basic fact of employment.

Due to industrial adjustment, employment restructuring, and changes in working-hour arrangements, laborers' working hours are liable to change in two ways under the new economy.

One is that laborers' working hours will remain high and working overtime will continue. This is because, under the new economy, the tertiary industry—particularly the country's constantly expanding modern services—provides more job opportunities than the primary and secondary industries, and laborers are more inclined to work in the tertiary industry. Yet in terms of weekly working hours, the tertiary industry is much longer than the primary and secondary industries. Therefore, working hours in the tertiary industry—especially in those service sectors closely related to high technology—will remain at a high level and will likely continue to exceed 40 hours a week.

A markedly different situation might be a shortening of laborers' working hours. Along with an increase in flexible employment, innovation, entrepreneurship, and new forms of employment, the current working hours and workplaces are also more flexible than in the past. To a certain degree, this can reduce the time laborers are required to commute—in particular those working in megacities—and thus can shorten laborers' working hours in the broader sense. Meanwhile, flexible and innovative work models no longer rely on long hours and high-intensity labor, but, rather, an increase in productivity through the improvement of human capital and working efficiency. In this way, laborers can reduce their working hours through more high-tech or innovative means than previously, and subsequently spend the time they saved investing in human capital, promoting their innovative and creative capacities, and adapting themselves to the ever-increasing demands on laborers' quality under the new economy.

---

10    Source: *China Labor Statistical Yearbooks* 2012–2015.

### 2.3 *Changes in the Way Laborers Work*

When we speak of "ways of working," we may mean many things. In this chapter, we will analyze the changes in laborers' working conditions under the new economy in light of their workplaces, ways of working, and work contents.

First, let's look at the changes in laborers' workplaces.

Currently, most laborers in China work in a fixed place, which corresponds with a fixed working-hour arrangement. In general, laborers must gather at the workplace and finish their work tasks there, and they are not allowed to decide where to work. Except for special sectors and professions, the majority of laborers work in a fixed place and are usually expected to complete the work within that location. As different types of work are usually separated, there is little overlap among different workplaces. To some degree, fixed workplaces tend to limit the development of laborers' creative and innovative capacities.

Under the new economy, with the development of science and technology—especially the constant development of the internet and computers—workplace flexibility will increase. A growing number of enterprises—in particular service and smart product providers—no longer require their employees to work at a fixed place. Rather, they allow their employees to work anywhere under the condition that the latter make good use of the corporate resources available to them and accomplish the designated tasks. Consequently, under the new economy, a growing number of laborers will choose a new pattern of work—namely, remote work by use of high-tech means. Meanwhile, their workplaces will also evolve from functioning as a single office towards a model of co-working spaces. Through construction design, technical support, and functional development, it is possible to integrate the office, leisure time, and life in one workplace, to build a more comfortable set of working condition to meet the various needs of employees, and to improve employees' creativity and efficiency.

Next, let's look at the changes in the forms of work.

China's labor market currently allows for many different forms of employment, such as formal employment, informal employment, flexible employment, and the emerging new forms of employment that are the subject of this chapter. This has given rise to various forms of work among Chinese laborers. For a long time, formal employees have made up the major labor force in China. With the development of new economic conditions, however, China's industrial and employment structure is constantly changing, and China's informal and flexible employment is developing very rapidly as a result. Scholars' views on the statistical scope and calculations of informal employment are not completely consistent, but they tend to agree that the proportion and number of informal employees are both very high.[11]

The new economy boasts a great diversity of work forms available to laborers, including flexible laborers without a fixed employer (e.g., odd job or hourly workers); laborers with a fixed employer but without a labor contract and without social insurance paid by the employer; laborers with stable employment plus additional, flexible part-time jobs (e.g., Didi drivers); and freelancers that do not belong to any organization and do not make long-term promises to any employer (e.g., Taobao shopkeepers). This is probably because of an uneven distribution of factors—such as data, information, and knowledge—available to different individuals. With the arrival of the "Internet Plus" Age and the Big Data Era, social collaboration has become common on a large scale, wherein different factors are integrated and utilized in order for individuals and companies to operate together.

What's more, China's progress in the field of information technology and its rapid development has provided room for efficient approaches to innovation and entrepreneurship. Innovation and entrepreneurship will become typical forms of employment in the future. The scalable and flexible infrastructure facilities brought about by public clouds and sharing platforms, the low-cost market promotional approaches brought about by mobile social media, the sales channels provided by internet platforms, the low-threshold financing channels provided by online finance, and the government's formulation and implementation of a series of relevant policies, all these have facilitated laborers' choice of innovation and entrepreneurship as a new form of employment.

Finally, let's look at the ongoing changes to the contents of the work itself.

Given the current progress of science and technology and declining transaction costs, the social division of labor is becoming increasingly specific, traditional professions are being divided and re-divided, and numerous jobs representing new forms and new contents are being created. Under such circumstances, the contents of work are increasingly detailed and abundant. For example, based on the internet and the exchange of big data, some innovative services are being developed to meet the specific needs of consumers, such as

---

11    Wu Yaowu and Cai Fang 吴要武、蔡昉, "Zhongguo chengzhen fei zhenggui jiuye guimo yu tezheng 中国城镇非正规就业:规模与特征 [Informal Employment in Urban China: Size and Characteristics]," *China Labor Economics* 2 (2006): 67–84. Xue Jinjun and Gao Wenshu 薛进军、高文书, "Zhongguo chengzhen fei zhenggui jiuye guimo tezheng yu shouru chaju 中国城镇非正规就业:规模、特征和收入差距 [Informal Employment in Urban China: Size, Characteristics, and income gap]," *Comparative Economic & Social Systems* 6 (2012): 59–69.

the wake-up call, the apology service, the web camera, etc. These are new types of work content that workers can choose to pursue. Meanwhile, and more specifically, new professions are emerging to satisfy consumers' new demands and provide them with new experiences. For example, highly professional jobs are emerging one after another, such as the "Flash Express" for fresh food delivery and the "Storager" for wardrobe sorting. What's more, in order to adapt to the new kinds of work, laborers have to make technical progress, and this has, in turn, enriched their working means and methods. For example, different application platforms (such as computers, the MAC system, the Android system, and the iOS system) require different technical means for implementation. Even the development of the same app can require different programmers— an "app technical engineer"—for development, programming, administration, and maintenance. Undoubtedly, it can improve laborers' work efficiency and effectiveness if they make good use of AI, information platforms, and machine learning, and ultimately dig deeply into the vast sea of information and data.

## 3 Changes in Labor Relations under the New Economy

### 3.1 *Current Condition of Labor Relations in China*

With the deepening of China's reforms, the adjustment of its industrial structure, and the ongoing changes to its model of economic growth, labor relations are changing in the country. Currently in China, labor standards are being perfected, labor relations are increasingly stable, and the coordination mechanism for labor relations is sounder than ever before.

To start with, a complete system of labor laws has been established, the coordinating system for laws and regulations related to labor relations is being constantly improved, and relevant legislations and their implementations are having remarkable effects. This legal system is grounded and centered on the *Labor Law of the People's Republic of China* (hereafter referred to as the *Labor Law*), supplemented with the *Labor Contract Law of the People's Republic of China* (hereafter referred to as the *Labor Contract Law*), the *Law of the People's Republic of China on Social Insurance*, the *Employment Promotion Law of the People's Republic of China*, the *Law of the People's Republic of China on Labor Dispute Mediation and Arbitration*, and the *Law of the People's Republic of China on Trade Unions* (hereafter referred to as the *Trade Unions Law*), and supported by administrative regulations and rules from related departments. It has effectively and substantially safeguarded the basic labor rights and the interests of laborers in China. The implementation of such laws and regulations has facilitated the stability of labor relations in the country. For example, since the implementation of the *Labor Contract Law* in 2008, there has been a significant increase in labor contracts signed and fulfilled between employers and laborers, as well as a significant reduction in short-term labor contracts. Meanwhile, there has also been a significant increase in the rate at which labor contracts are signed at the same time that the contents of labor contracts have become increasingly standardized. According to statistics, from the end of 2011 to the end of 2015, the labor-contract signing rate of enterprises in China was 86.4 percent, 88.4 percent, 88.2 percent, 88 percent, and 90 percent, annually.[12]

Secondly, the role of labor dispute settlement mechanisms is being constantly reinforced, which includes sustaining labor relation stability and protecting laborers' rights and interests. Over the past decade, there has been a significant increase in the number of disputes handled by labor and personnel dispute arbitration institutions in China. By use of mediation, arbitration, and other means, the number of disputes settled has increased significantly. In 2015, 813,859 disputes were accepted by labor and personnel dispute arbitration institutions that concerned 1,159,687 laborers, with 812,461 of those disputes being settled.[13] In 2016, 828,714 disputes were accepted by labor and personnel dispute arbitration institutions with 1,112,375 laborers concerned, and 827,889 of those disputes were settled.[14] Dispute settlement rates have seen a significant increase from 92.3 percent in 2005 to 95.2 percent in 2015 (See Figure 3.2).

Third, labor relations in China are increasingly market-based. Since the country's reform and opening up, a pattern known as public ownership has become China's mainstay along with the joint development of diverse forms of ownership. The labor relations seen in non-public enterprises (i.e., market-dominated sectors) are typically market-based, and they are usually determined by the labor market, the power of the market economy, and the country's labor laws and regulations. Yet within a market-oriented labor relationship, there are always contradictions and conflicts of interest between the employer and the employee, due to inadequate communication between them. On the other hand, the laborer's awareness of how to safeguard his/her rights is not adequately developed, and the need to strengthen labor security remains. Consequently, market-based labor relations are prone to disputes and conflict and are marked by a lack of harmony. What's more, the labor relations seen in public sectors of the Chinese economy are gradually being integrated

---

12    *Statistical Bulletin on the Development of the Human Resources and Social Security* (2011–2015).

13    *China Statistical Yearbook* (2016).

14    *Human Resources and Social Security Statistical Express Data 2016.*

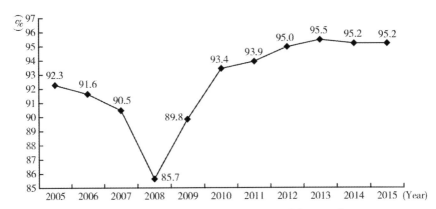

FIGURE 3.2   Dispute settlement rates of labor and personnel dispute arbitration institutions (2005–2015)
SOURCE: CALCULATED BY THE AUTHOR USING STATISTICS PROVIDED IN *CHINA STATISTICAL YEARBOOKS* (2015–2016).

with the market, and conflicts of interest between employers and employees are also beginning to manifest. Therefore, labor relations in public sectors cannot be considered conflict-free.

Finally, as changes are taking place among labor relations, China's labor unions are developing rapidly and continue to play an important role in protecting laborers' rights and interests within the new framework of labor relations. By the end of 2015, there were 2.806 million grassroots trade unions in China, covering 307 million laborers, including 295 million trade union members.[15] At present, labor unions in China have grown from state-owned enterprises to non-public enterprises, covering not only employees in the public sectors of the Chinese economy, but also other types of workers, such as migrant workers and employees of transnational companies. This has enabled the country's labor unions to play a larger role in protecting laborers' rights and interests across a broad range of issues. In 2014, taking into account all corporate trade union members, 25.946 million worked in state-owned enterprises, 8.274 million in collective-owned enterprises, 103 million in private enterprises, 8.358 million in Hong Kong, Macao, and Taiwan-funded enterprises, and 9.805 million in foreign-funded enterprises.[16] In 2015, 15 million migrant workers became trade union members; in 2016, another 15 million

---

15    *China Statistical Yearbook* (2016).
16    *China Labor Statistical Yearbook 2015*.

AN ANALYSIS OF THE CHANGES TO LABOR RELATIONS 57

migrant workers joined labor unions. Thus, trade union members accounted for over 50 percent of all migrant workers nationwide.[17]

### 3.2 Changes in Labor Relations under the New Economy

Under the new economy, labor relations will keep improving in China, and protection for laborers will be constantly strengthened. At the same time, a number of new problems are emerging. Under China's new economic conditions, some problems are becoming increasingly prominent, such as the difference in modes of employment, the relatively wide gap between different types of laborers in terms of wages, benefits, and social insurance, the problem of migrant workers, and the mismatch between the country's current institutions and new forms of employment that are emerging under the sharing economy. The following are our predictions for the major changes in labor relations in China under the new economy.

The first change is that, with the development of the new economy and new employment, modes of employment are changing, and there will be various forms of labor relations that emerge in addition to the conventional ones. Different from the fixed and long-term labor relations of formal employees, the labor relations of flexible employees—such as part-time workers, temporary contract workers, and hourly workers—are more diversified and are usually informal, dynamic, and short-term. Specifically, there are probably three major forms of labor relations as follows.

First, labor relations directly established between laborers and conventional employers and in the form of labor contracts. This type of labor relationship has long been dominant in formal employment as well as informal jobs that are long-term and fixed. As many of the country's current laws and institutions are employer-based, such directly-established labor relations are better protected by the law, which is an effective guarantee for laborers' rights and interests. Within such a labor relationship, the laborer connects with the employer through the market, exchanges value, and obtains remuneration from the employer. Yet conflicts of interest, contradiction, and labor disputes in this type of labor relationship are always directly between the employer and the laborer.

Second, short-term, flexible employment by enterprises is developing rapidly. This form of labor relationship increases the number of informal and flexible employees through intermediaries, e.g., human resources service institutions, which help employ laborers who then provide services and complete

17    http://acftu.workercn.cn/34/201701/18/170118071348760.shtml.

the work.[18] In such a form of employment, the relation between the employer and the employees depends on how much work and power the employer has outsourced through the intermediary.

Third, the relationship between different parties on the labor market represents a new form of employment under the sharing economy. The position-oriented work forms that previously existed under the traditional economy are being replaced by task-oriented work relations under the new economy. Within such a relationship, laborers are not under the direct control of employers, but are directly linked to the market through a platform for value exchange. This can somewhat reduce conflicts and contradictions, but under the current situation—in which relevant institutions have not adapted to the new economy and new employment currently developing in China—such laborers' rights and interests may not be well protected.

The characteristics of both sides of labor relations (employers and laborers) would possibly change. On the one hand, the size of employers can vary. Some enterprises are poised to continue growing, such as internet-based sharing economy platforms, while small- and micro-sized enterprises will grow in number, if not scale. Yet small- and micro-sized enterprises are the key fields of labor relations work due to the frequent occurrence of violations in them, such as labor disputes and the poor protection of laborers, because they are small in size and number of employees, fast in terms of employee mobility, and poor in human resource management and the handling of labor relations. Moreover, many non-legal entities—such as individuals, families, partnerships and other unincorporated subjects—have also joined the labor market as "employers." Given that such "employers" are outside the market's regulatory framework, they have made it difficult to fulfill labor contracts as well as to enforce any degree of supervision over labor security.

On the other hand, under the new economy, employment is more flexible and poses a lower barrier to entry, and laborers are less likely to be subject to employment discrimination. For example, entrepreneurship is a feasible form of employment for many people. It is relatively low in cost and is basically free from geographical restrictions. Therefore, some groups that have encountered difficulties in traditional forms of employment, such as women, older laborers, and young people who lack previous work experience, can find employment by

---

18　Xiong Jian 熊坚, "Renli ziben shidai duoyuan laodong guanxi qianxi 人力资本时代多元劳动关系浅析 [On Labor Relations in the Human Capital Era]," *China Labor* 1 (2017): 18–20.

starting up their own businesses. Furthermore, as new forms of employment are more open and inclusive than traditional jobs, they provide different groups of laborers with more equal job opportunities and employment earnings. With the increase of new-employment laborers, however, labor relations will become more complex. For example, a laborer may have established different types of labor relations with several employers. In this case, it will be more complicated to protect the laborer's rights and interests and to deal with labor disputes when/if they arise. Moreover, before corresponding institutions are created to support them, such laborers will have to risk income instability and the lack of employment protection, which heightens the instability of such labor relations.

Another type of change is that laborers working in jobs categorized as informal employment, flexible employment, and new forms of employment under the sharing economy are faced with many problems in attempting to protect their rights and interests, e.g., the non-applicability of some labor laws or regulations to their cases, imperfect mechanisms by which to settle labor disputes, and a lack of effective labor supervision, all of which have made it more difficult to protect their rights and interests.

Currently in China, almost all laws, regulations, and institutions related to the protection of laborers' rights and interests are based on labor contracts or formal labor relations, and their implementation depends to a great extent on employers. Yet such a practice is quite different from the case of laborers working under conditions of informal employment, flexible employment, and new forms of employment. In fact, it is rather difficult for such laborers to receive the current benefits of labor protection. For example, social insurance, endowment insurance, and medical insurance in China are generally based on labor contracts and have certain requirements for both the employee and the employer, who are sometimes required to pay insurance premiums according to the employee's income level. In informal employment and new forms of employment, however, labor relations are usually loose, which makes it difficult to measure—to even establish at all—a laborers' income level. Consequently, some laborers may be ineligible to enroll in social insurance, endowment insurance, and/or medical insurance. What's more, different regions can vary in the stipulation and implementation of their protection of laborers' rights and interests. Yet under the new economy, some laborers' employment and work are flexible and mobile, and it is thus likely that they will work or change their jobs frequently. This regional diversity in the protection of laborers' rights and interests heightens the difficulty of equally applying insurance to all employees.

Finally, according to stipulations outlined in the *Trade Unions Law*, the way the country's current labor unions are organized fits well with the terms of formal employment. Yet due to legal restrictions, some informal and flexible employees are not able to join labor unions and many laborers newly employed under the new economy and new models of business find it difficult to be accepted or covered by labor unions. With the development of the new economy, informal employment and new employment will increase further, but the current labor union system is having a negative effect on the establishment of labor unions' organization, the unions' representation of laborers, and the protection of the rights and interests of informal, flexible, and new -employment laborers.

## 4 Suggestions on the Development of Labor Relations under the New Economy

Under the new economy, new forms of employment are growing rapidly and the labor relations of Chinese laborers are constantly changing. For example, their working hours are more flexible, liberal, and fragmented, and are most likely becoming shorter despite remaining relatively high overall. Laborers' workplaces are flexible and variable in space, their jobs take various forms and are rich in content, and they use high-tech working methods. Under the new economy, labor relations are faced with new changes and challenges in terms of the forms and subjects of labor relations as well as the protection of laborers' rights and interests. Therefore, in order to adapt to new changes and new requirements, we must adopt new approaches to develop labor relations under the new economy and to more effectively guarantee China's economic growth and industrial upgrading in the future.

### 4.1 *Strengthen the Management and Utilization of Working Hours*
Under the new economy, laborers have more freedom in their working hours, which are structured around fragmented tasks and information. Accordingly, it is necessary for both employers and laborers to manage these flexible working hours, to make corresponding alterations to the continuity, concentration, and goal-orientation of the working hours, and to reduce ineffective working hours by adopting new approaches towards their working-hour arrangements.

On the one hand, employers must help laborers adapt to new changes in their working hours by adopting the following measures.

First of all, in the overall working environment, employers must reduce those factors that might interfere with employees. For example, they must formulate rules regarding communication, adopt less intrusive means of communication—such as emails and texts—for non-urgent affairs, and have meetings at the beginning or at the end of the workday. All these measures are conducive to the continuity of and concentration during working hours.

Secondly, employers must give their employees some degree of freedom over their own time management and autonomy in workplace tasks. For example, they may allow their employees—insofar as it doesn't affect their work—to make their own arrangements about tasks, schedules, and relevant affairs within working hours. When it comes to certain flexible but not urgent tasks, employers would do well to allow their employees to make more reasonable arrangements. For example, employees must be permitted to break a task down into smaller parts and spend large blocks of time focused on other matters. What the employers should do in this situation, then, is limit their focus to a control of the time and quality of completion.

Thirdly, employers must make good use of fragmented or discrete units of time to communicate with their employees and arrange employees' training and other work-related affairs. Meanwhile, using internet technology, they can display teaching material and display training courses using a network platform, or use that same platform to communicate with employees. In this way, they can flexibly embed into the employees' working hours activities that traditional require large blocks of time, so as to improve working efficiency and flexibility.

That being said, laborers must themselves adopt certain approaches to more effectively take advantage of such changes in their working hours.

Firstly, laborers must focus on the current task within a given block of time. They must not multitask simultaneously or shift between tasks within that time. For example, shifting between sending and receiving emails, answering the phone, and preparing work reports, all within the span of one hour, increases laborers' pressure and therefore lowers their working efficiency, which is adverse to the completion of work tasks.

Secondly, laborers must make investments in human capital and improve their labor skills by making good use of break time and integrating the fragmented and flexible time they have between work tasks. For example, laborers may arrange other kinds of tasks for themselves during their break time. They may pursue knowledge that is relevant to their work, ponder what can be improved in their work, accumulate fragmented information, and adjust their mood and state of mind in order to adapt to the next work task.

Thirdly, for freelancers or part-time laborers, it is all the more important to adequately arrange the schedule of different work tasks and ensure both efficiency and quality across all tasks. This requires laborers to have a solid grasp of their work—especially how much time each task takes, whether the work tasks on hand can be flexibly arranged, whether there is a possibility to make changes, etc. Only when they are intimately familiar with such conditions can laborers make overarching plans for their limited time and arrange their tasks reasonably and effectively.

### 4.2 Promote the Integrated Development of Both Traditional and New Forms of Employment

Under the new economy, changes in work methods are closely related to changes in the form employment takes. In the future, we must promote the coexistence and development of both traditional and new forms of employment as well as the integration of traditional and flexible work methods.

As work methods are developing toward increased flexibility and diversity, employers must no longer require laborers to meet traditional standards, such as fixed working hours and fixed workplaces. On the contrary, they must create differentiated standards based on the specific conditions of different industries and sectors, so as to boost the integrated development of new work methods alongside more traditional forms.

To begin with, institutionally, employers must strengthen the internal compulsory constraints on new-employment laborers. Meanwhile, government sectors may adopt certain external compulsory constraints from the traditional economy and conduct external supervision of new-employment laborers. The internal compulsory constraints of new forms of employment include automatic and intelligent constraints within the platform and self-supervision. The external compulsory constraints taken from the traditional economy include laws and regulations—such as commercial law, tax law, and banking laws—and supporting policies. By doing so, it is possible to boost the integration of different forms of employment and to promote new methods of working though formal channels.

Secondly—and technically—it is advisable to integrate and develop industrial technology (which is used to improve productivity in the traditional economy) and information technology and data technology (which are used to improve trading capacity under the new economy and among new models of business). Under the new economy, it is necessary to combine various technologies together, such as the internet, machine intelligence, and big-data analysis, so as to improve both productivity and trading capacity, and facilitate the structural upgrading of different industries.

Finally, in terms of information exchange, the government and private enterprises may create chances for laborers in both the traditional economy and those operating under new employment standards to communicate with

AN ANALYSIS OF THE CHANGES TO LABOR RELATIONS                                    63

each other. For example, different types of laborers may share their experiences, technology, and resources on new-employment platforms, systems, and through other means that are conducive to resource sharing. Laborers within the traditional economy may break down the existing institutional and structural barriers and become new-employment laborers as part-time, cross-industrial, or cross-platform workers. These measures will enable laborers currently on the labor market to exchange and share the overall labor capacity and human capital they possess, which would help such laborers improve their skills.

### 4.3    Clarify Labor Relations under the New Economy and Enhance the Stability of Labor Relations

First of all, it is necessary to clarify the relevant content of labor relations and protect the lawful rights and interests of each party—in particular those of laborers. Traditionally, there are usually three standards stipulating the establishment of labor relations between employers and employees:[19]

1.    Both the employer and laborer are lawful entities.
2.    The labor regulations and rules formulated by the employer apply to the laborer, who is subject to the employer's labor management and is engaged in paid labor arranged by the employer.
3.    The labor provided by the employee is part of the employer's business.

These three standards define formal labor relations and some informal labor relations and can be applied when handling relevant issues. Yet with the emergence of informal employment, new methods of work, and new forms of employment, these standards have become less able to adapt to the current reality of diversified labor relations.

Secondly, under the new economy, the complexity of labor relations affects their stability. Both the government and employers must endeavor to enhance the stability of labor relations. Employers—especially small- and micro-sized enterprises—must strengthen the management of labor relations and formulate practical measures to solve the problems currently affecting labor relations. In particular, many microenterprises are developing rapidly and have become major fields for employment, but they have not been established for long. As such, they are relatively high in terms of employee mobility and their working, production, and business conditions have not fully matured. In order to stabilize labor relations, it is necessary for such enterprises to adopt

---

19    On May 25, 2005, the former Ministry of Labour and Social Security published the *Notice on Issues Related to the Establishment of Labor Relations* [Notice No. (2015) 12]. http://www.mohrss.gov.cn/ldgxs/LDGXzhengcefagui/LDGXzyzc/201107/t20110728_86296.htm.

some countermeasures to settle the existing problems facing labor relations. For example, they must refine the contents of labor contracts, improve social security measures, improve both workplace and production environments, and appropriately adjust their wage structures.

Finally, it is necessary to modify existing laws and regulations related to labor unions, adjust the organization of and mechanisms by which labor unions function, strengthen the governance capacity of labor unions, and continue to foreground the role of labor unions, so as to adapt to the development of the new economy and new employment.

In order that laborers working under the aegis of informal employment, flexible employment, and new employment can join labor unions, the legislature must appropriately revise the existing *Trade Unions Law* and other related laws, such as the stipulations outlining labor unions' organization and institutions, which entities are entitled to enroll in and organize labor unions, restrictions on the employers of laborers participating in and organizing labor unions, and more.[20] Meanwhile, it is time for China to overcome the limitations on the organization of traditional labor unions and establish industrial trade unions, especially in sectors with new forms of employment, such as the telecommunications industry. Using new technologies, such as the internet and big-data technologies, newly founded trade unions can collect and analyze the data and conditions specific to sectoral employment. On that basis, it is possible to standardize and formulate sectoral and industrial labor standards, collective wage coordination mechanisms, contract normative mechanisms, and more.[21] It is also feasible to promote trade union services by means of new information technology, so as to protect the rights and interests of informal and new-employment laborers. That being said, for their part, labor unions in China must alter their methods and philosophy insofar as it relates to work and innovate their working concepts, and also establish corporate labor unions in new employment enterprises using large internet-based platforms. For smaller enterprises and flexibly employed laborers, labor unions must provide relevant services. They must double down on their services for laborers working within informal, flexible, and new employment positions, and also increase their coverage of new types of labor relations.

---

20 Zhu Dongli 朱懂理, "Shilun feizhenggui jiuye dui zhongguo gonghui zuzhi tizhi de yingxiang yu yingdui 试论非正规就业对中国工会组织体制的影响与应对 [On the Influence of Informal Employment on the Institution of China's Labor Unions and Countermeasures]," *Journal of China University of Labor Relations* 2 (2013):50–53.

21 Ji Wenwen and Lai Desheng 纪雯雯、赖德胜, "Wangluo pingtai jiuye dui laodongguanxi de yingxiang jizhi yu shijian fenxi 网络平台就业对劳动关系的影响机制与实践分析 [The Influence Mechanism of Employment of Online Platforms on Labor Relations: An Empirical Analysis]," *Journal of China University of Labor Relations* 4 (2016):6–16.

## Author Biography

Xie Qianyun has a Ph.D. and research assistant at the CASS Institute of Population and Labor Economics. Her academic interests includes labor economics and human resource management.

## References

Guo Tongxin 郭同欣, "Gaige chuanxin chujin le woguo jiuye chixu kuoda 改革创新促进了我国就业持续扩大 [Reform and Innovation Boost China's Sustained Employment Growth]," *People's Daily*, March 29, 2017.

Ji Wenwen and Lai Desheng 纪雯雯、赖德胜, "Wangluo pingtai jiuye dui laodongguanxi de yingxiang jizhi yu shijian fenxi 网络平台就业对劳动关系的影响机制与实践分析 [The Influence Mechanism of Employment of Online Platforms on Labor Relations: An Empirical Analysis]," *Journal of China University of Labor Relations* 4 (2016): 6–16.

Lai Desheng, Meng Dahu, Wang Qi 赖德胜、孟大虎、王琦, "Woguo laodongzhe gongzuo shijian tezheng yu zhengce xuanze 我国劳动者工作时间特征与政策选择 [Characteristics of Chinese Laborers' Working Hours and Policy Choices]," *China Labor* 2 (2015): 36–40.

Liu Shusheng and Li Shi 刘树成、李实, "Dui meiguo xin jingji de kaocha yu yanjiu 对美国"新经济"的考察与研究 [Observation and Studies on the New Economy in the US]," *Economic Research Journal* 8 (2000): 3–11, 55–79.

Wu Yaowu and Cai Fang 吴要武、蔡昉, "Zhongguo chengzhen fei zhenggui jiuye guimo yu tezheng 中国城镇非正规就业：规模与特征 [Informal Employment in Urban China: Size and Characteristics]," *China Labor Economics* 2 (2006): 67–84.

Xiang Xiaomei 向晓梅, "Shiying xin changtai fazhan xin jingji 适应新常态发展新经济 [Adapt to the New Normal and Develop the New Economy]," *Economic Daily*, May 5, 2016.

Xiong Jian 熊坚, "Renli ziben shidai duoyuan laodong guanxi qianxi 人力资本时代多元劳动关系浅析 [On Labor Relations in the Human Capital Era]," *China Labor* 1 (2017): 18–20.

Xue Jinjun and Gao Wenshu 薛进军、高文书, "Zhongguo chengzhen fei zhenggui jiuye guimo tezheng yu shouru chaju 中国城镇非正规就业：规模、特征和收入差距 [Informal Employment in Urban China: Size, Characteristics, and income gap]," *Comparative Economic & Social Systems* 6 (2012): 59–69.

Zhang Chenggang 张成刚, "Jiuye fazhan de weilai qushi xin jiuye xingtai de gainian ji yingxiang fenxi 就业发展的未来趋势，新就业形态的概念及影响分析 [The Future Trend of Employment development and the Concept and Influence of New Employment]," *Human Resources Development of China* 19 (2016).

Zhang Juwei 张车伟, "Shibada yilai woguo jiuye xin tedian he jiuye youxian zhanlüe xin neihan 十八大以来我国就业新特点和就业优先战略新内涵 [New Characteristics of China's Employment Since the 18th CPC National Congress and New Connotations of the Employment Priority Strategy]," *People's Daily*, July 19, 2017.

Zhu Dongli 朱懂理, "Shilun feizhenggui jiuye dui zhongguo gonghui zuzhi tizhi de yingxiang yu yingdui 试论非正规就业对中国工会组织体制的影响与应对 [On the Influence of Informal Employment on the Institution of China's Labor Unions and Countermeasures]," *Journal of China University of Labor Relations* 2 (2013): 50–53.

CHAPTER 4

# Employment and Work on Online Ride-Hailing Platforms: a Study of Didi Platform Data

*Wu Qingjun, Yang Weiguo, Wang Qi, and Chen Xiaofei*

## 1 Research Background and Explanation of Data

### 1.1 *Research Background and Objectives*

In July 2017, the National Development and Reform Commission, together with seven other government authorities, published the *Guiding Opinions on Promoting the Development of the Sharing Economy*. The *Opinions* clearly points to the fact that the development of the sharing economy will effectively improve the utilization efficiency of social resources and facilitate the improvement of people's lives, which is of profound importance to China's supply-side reforms, the implementation of the country's innovation-driven development strategy, the promotion of mass entrepreneurship and innovation, and the cultivation of a new momentum for China's economic development. According to the *China Sharing Economy Development Report 2017*, issued by China's State Information Center, transactions made through China's sharing-economy market totaled RMB 3,452 billion in 2016, including traffic transactions of RMB 203.8 billion. Meanwhile, the rapid growth of the sharing economy has changed previous traditional methods of employment and created numerous flexible job opportunities. In 2016, 0.6 billion people took part in a sharing-economy activity, with approximately 60 million service providers—including 18.55 million in the field of traffic and travel.

With the rapid development of its innovation and entrepreneurship, China's sharing economy has demonstrated an enormous vitality and potential for development. Yet the sharing economy is currently faced with numerous problems and challenges, such as inconsistencies, inadequate institutions, and insufficient social security.[1] Of the many problems discussed herein,

---

1 As noted in the *Guiding Opinions on Promoting the Development of the Sharing Economy*, China's innovative and entrepreneurial sharing economy has been developing rapidly in recent years; by taking advantage of "Internet Plus," it has created many new models of business, helped resolve overcapacity in China, created numerous new jobs, and displayed enormous vitality and potential for development. The sharing economy has become key to the wider and more in-depth development of mass entrepreneurship and innovation, as well

© KONINKLIJKE BRILL NV, LEIDEN, 2020 | DOI:10.1163/9789004435803_005

the relationship between employees and platform enterprises, as well as the relevant labor security protections tied to both, remains vague in academic circles. In order to further study laborers' job characteristics and labor relations under the sharing economy, from May to August 2017, a research group under the School of Labor and Human Resources, Renmin University of China, conducted in-depth research on the job characteristics and labor relations of drivers utilizing the Didi online ride-hailing platform, a representative platform of China's sharing economy.

Through this research, the research group hopes to achieve four objectives. Firstly, we hope to describe and analyze the representative characteristics of Didi drivers and position both part-time and full-time drivers on the social structure. Secondly, we intend to describe and analyze the job characteristics of Didi drivers, as well as summarize and define the job characteristics under the sharing economy. Thirdly, we intend to perform an in-depth analysis of Didi drivers' work nature and working relations and expound upon the working relations between Didi drivers and the various organizations that are established at work. Finally, we will analyze and predict the orientation of online ride-hailing drivers' career in the future, and put forward some suggestions corresponding to institutional design.

## 1.2 *Sample Data Descriptions*

In order to accurately describe online ride-hailing operations and the drivers' working conditions, the research group carried out field investigations and large-sample questionnaire surveys for data collection.

From December 2016 to May 2017, the group made field surveys at Didi headquarters and in Beijing, Shenzhen, Quanzhou, and Chengdu. The subjects of the survey include the management of major Didi operating departments and branch offices, Didi Premier/Express drivers, leasing company management, taxi drivers, and taxi company management. The contents of the survey included the characteristics of drivers as a group, their working procedures, their working rules, their service objects, and operation typical of the local transportation market.

Based on field investigations, the research group designed a questionnaire and conducted the subsequent survey. We first drew one or two top-, middle-,

---

as "a new force" in China's economic and social development. Yet the sharing economy is currently faced with numerous problems and challenges such as inconsistencies, inadequate institutions, and insufficient social security.

and lower-ranking cities in terms of passenger capacity from every provincial-level division. The group then randomly selected 30 percent of all active drivers[2] and sent them the questionnaire as a cell phone text. Altogether, the research group received 30,671 valid questionnaires.

In order to better understand the job conditions inherent to and characteristics of online ride-hailing drivers, upon receiving the completed questionnaires, we cross-checked the responses against the data the Didi platform keeps on their drivers in order to ensure accuracy. Such data cover a broad range, including the driver's gender, age, years of driving experience, date and place of registration as a driver on Didi, the number of monthly ride orders, type of service (Express/Premier Driving) provided, the driver's relationship with Didi (independent contractor/corporate member/franchise), the driver's service score, the number of monthly ride orders, the car's monthly mileage, number of driving hours a month, number of online availability hours a month, monthly income, the number of times cited in complaints, vehicle age, vehicle make (e.g., Toyota Corolla), the prevailing vehicle price (pre-tax), the prevailing vehicle price (after tax), the wheel base, the engine displacement, the number of seats, horsepower, and the license plate number (the first three letters/numbers).

We also collected the data of the number of monthly ride orders, monthly mileage, number of driving hours a month, number of online availability hours a month, monthly income from June 2016 to June 2017 (13 months), the number of times cited in complaints from January 1 to June 18 of 2017, and all other indicators on June 18, 2017.

## 2      Characteristics of Online Ride-Hailing Drivers

### 2.1      *Basic Characteristics of Online Ride-Hailing Drivers*
2.1.1      The Total Number of Drivers
According to statistics provided by Didi Chuxing (Didi Travel), 21.078 million Didi drivers (of Didi Premier/Express, Hitch, and Designated Driving Service) have fulfilled at least one ride order on the platform over the past year (from August 2016 to August 2017), accounting for 6.2 percent of the total employment

---

2  "Active drivers" refer to drivers who took at least one ride order on the platform between January and June 2017.

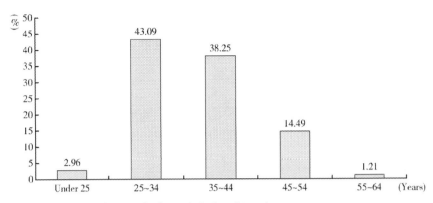

FIGURE 4.1   Distribution of online ride-hailing drivers by age

in China's tertiary industry at the end of 2016,[3] six percentage points higher than in the previous statistical period.[4]

2.1.2     Age

As we find in the survey, the sample of drivers covers all age-groups (from "below 25" to "55–64"), but most of them are young people aged "25–34" and "35–44," accounting for 43.09 percent and 38.25 percent of all drivers, respectively. Obviously, with its low threshold for age requirements, the online ride-hailing platform has provided a job opportunity for participants from every age group.

2.1.3     Gender

In terms of their gender, the majority of ride-hailing drivers are men, accounting for 95.91 percent of all surveyed rideshare drivers, while women accounted for only a small number of drivers, making up 4.09 percent of the rideshare force. Back-end statistics show that there are 1.365 million female ride-hailing drivers.[5]

---

3   According to China's Ministry of Human Resources and Social Security, total employment was 776.03 million people in 2016, of which the tertiary industry accounted of 43.5 percent (approximately 337.57 million people).
4   The previous statistical period refers to the year 2016. For further information, see the "Report on Employment Promotion by Car Hailing 2015–2016."
5   Since gender information is joined the platform, the back-end statistics are higher than the proportion we surveyed.

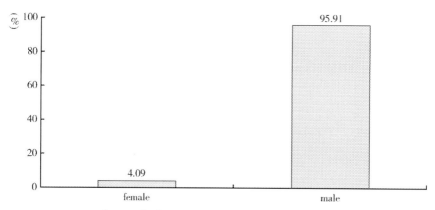

FIGURE 4.2    Distribution of online ride-hailing drivers by gender

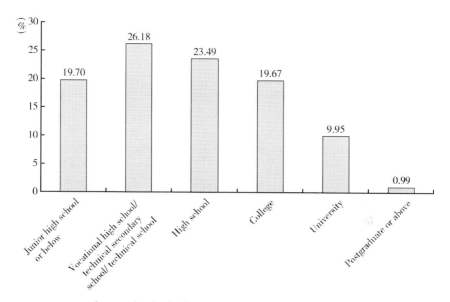

FIGURE 4.3    Education levels of online ride-hailing drivers

2.1.4    Education

In terms of educational level, ride-hailing drivers vary from "junior high school or below" to "postgraduate or above," with participants coming from almost all walks of life. This reflects the employment flexibility of online ride-hailing, which is free from the restrictions of education and social stratum. Most drivers have completed an education in a "vocational high school/technical secondary school/technical school" or a "high school," accounting for 26.18 percent and 23.49 percent of all surveyed participants, respectively.

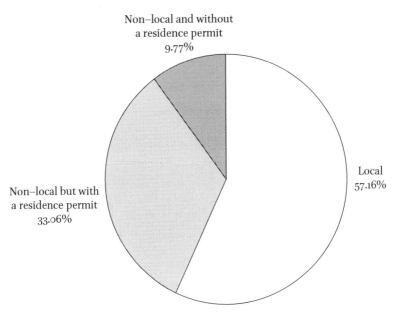

FIGURE 4.4    Household registration status of online ride-hailing drivers

### 2.1.5    Household Registration Status

According to our statistics taken on sample drivers, over half (57.16 percent) of online ride-hailing drivers are registered as local residents, while 33.06 percent are holders of a residence permit despite not being registered as local. The proportion of non-local drivers is relatively high in megacities such as Beijing (43.5 percent) and Shanghai (56.9 percent), where most drivers have a stable job in the city.

### 2.1.6    Full-Time versus Part-Time

Based on an evaluation of their working conditions, 63.28 percent of respondents indicated that they "have a job besides online ride-hailing,"[6] while 36.72 percent have indicated that they are a "full-time online ride-hailing driver." This shows that an increasing number of people from a variety of professional backgrounds are taking part in the sharing economy, and the larger the proportion of part-time ride-hailing drivers, the more typical this sector is of the sharing economy.

---

6   The proportion of part-time and full-time ride-hailing drivers comes from our questionnaire survey. According to the survey, 36.72 percent are full-time online ride-hailing drivers. Yet our interviews suggest a lower proportion of full-time online ride-hailing drivers. We assume that this is probably because the proportion of full-time ride-hailing drivers is too high in the samples of the questionnaire survey.

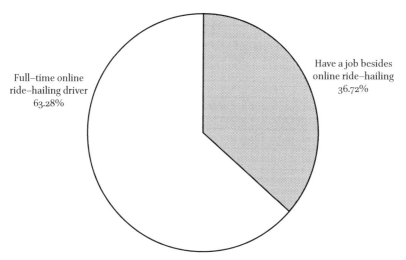

FIGURE 4.5    Working conditions of online ride-hailing drivers

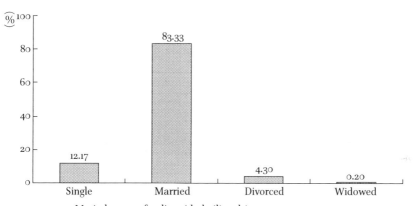

FIGURE 4.6    Marital status of online ride-hailing drivers

## 2.2    *Household, Income, and Expenditures of Online Ride-Hailing Drivers*
### 2.2.1    Household Structure

In terms of raising children, most online ride-hailing drivers shoulder a certain degree of family burden. Among our sample drivers, 83.33 percent are married and most have one child (51.22 percent) or two children (31.65 percent) under 18 (i.e., minor children, including stepchildren and adopted children). That is to say, most of them experience the pressure of child-rearing.

In terms of the number of household members and household employment, online ride-hailing drivers are faced with relatively heavy family burdens and are therefore dependent on the income they earn from the ridesharing

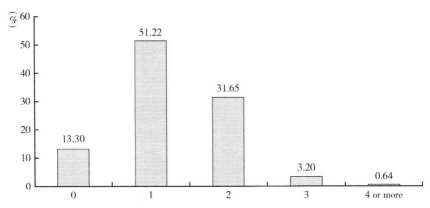

FIGURE 4.7　Number of minor children in online ride-hailing drivers' families

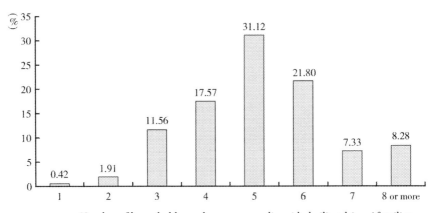

FIGURE 4.8　Number of household members among online ride-hailing drivers' families

platform. Most drivers have five (31.12 percent) or six (21.80) members in their family (immediate family members, including their parents, spouse, and children), yet among 49.11 percent of these families, only two members are employed.

2.2.2　Individual and Household Income and Expenditures

According to our statistics, the largest proportion (39.69 percent) of online ride-hailing drivers fall between RMB 3,000 and RMB 5,000 in terms of average individual monthly income; 23.54 percent pull in below RMB 3,000, and 20.38 percent between RMB 5,000 and RMB 7,000. Their income earned as online ride-hailing drivers plays a significant role in increasing their total individual income.

EMPLOYMENT AND WORK ON ONLINE RIDE-HAILING PLATFORMS 75

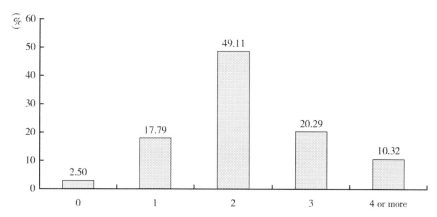

FIGURE 4.9  Number of employed household members among online ride-hailing drivers' families

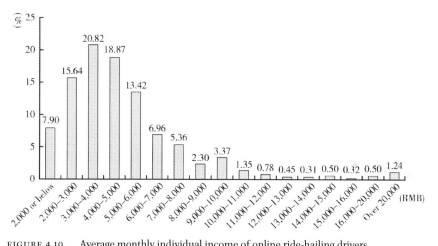

FIGURE 4.10  Average monthly individual income of online ride-hailing drivers

In terms of household income, online ride-hailing drivers are generally capable of making both ends meet with their income. Their monthly household income averages RMB 8,697.67, with 52.34 percent above RMB 7,000 and nearly half (47.66 percent) below RMB 7,000. Obviously, their overall income level is not high.

In terms of average monthly household expenditures, most sample drivers are able to make both ends meet and guarantee the basic necessities of life, with 35.41 percent of households averaging between RMB 3,000 and RMB 5,000 in monthly expenditures and 77.63 percent of households coming in below RMB 7,000.

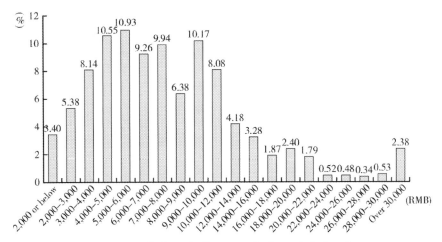

FIGURE 4.11    Average monthly household income of online ride-hailing drivers

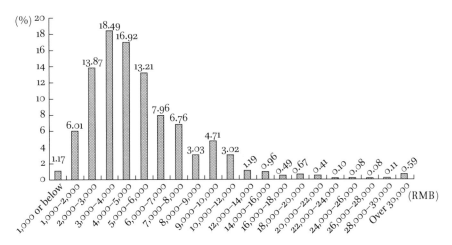

FIGURE 4.12    Average monthly household expenditures of online ride-hailing drivers

### 2.2.3    Property

In terms of property held in possession, most drivers registered as local residents own one or more properties. Their life is therefore stable, and their home ownership burden is relatively light. Most non-local drivers have no property in the city that they work in, and purchasing a house represents a big burden for them.

According to our statistics, 45.73 percent of sample drivers have no local property while 38.43 percent own one local property. Specifically, 76.31 percent of the local drivers have one or more local properties, 27.29 percent of the non-local drivers with a residence permit have at least one local property, and

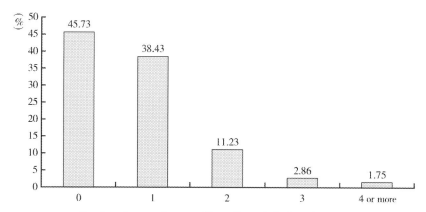

FIGURE 4.13    Number of properties owned by online ride-hailing drivers

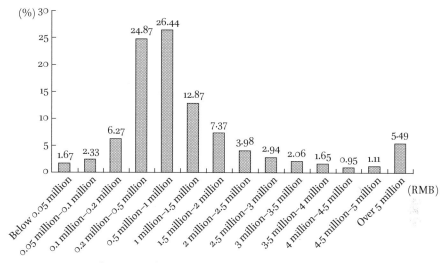

FIGURE 4.14    Local property value possessed by online ride-hailing drivers

only 16.18 percent of non-local drivers without a residence permit have a local property—they are the weakest in terms of their risk resistance.

Of those drivers possessing one or more local properties, 35.14 percent have a total value of less than RMB 0.5 million, 26.44 percent have a total value between RMB 0.5 million and RMB one million, and 32.93 percent have a total value between RMB one million and RMB five million.

2.2.4    Loans

According to our survey, 30.13 percent of rideshare drivers carry no loans at all and, in general, online ride-hailing drivers are relatively low in terms of carrying a burden of debt.

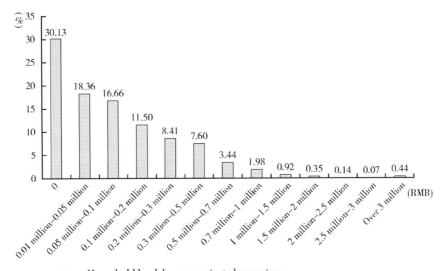

FIGURE 4.15    Household bank loans or private borrowings

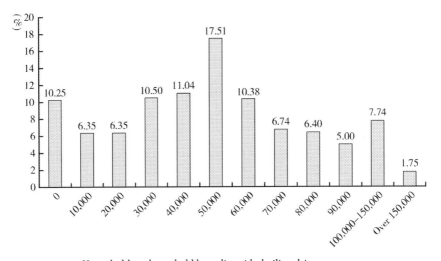

FIGURE 4.16    Household car loans held by online ride-hailing drivers

In terms of home bank loans or private loans, online ride-hailing drivers tend to only take out small loans and carry a light burden of debt, with 30.13 percent of drivers completely without loans or borrowings, and 35.02 percent having only borrowed RMB 10,000 to 100,000.

In terms of car loans, current levels are well within the drivers' financial capacities. According to our statistical analysis, 10.25 percent of the sample

EMPLOYMENT AND WORK ON ONLINE RIDE-HAILING PLATFORMS

drivers have no car loans, and 51.75 percent of them have car loans ranging from RMB 10,000 to RMB 50,000. Besides, these drivers can join online ride-sharing platforms with their private cars, which are otherwise idle resources. This reflects the low threshold to and low cost of the sharing economy.

After a general comparison of the sample drivers' income and expenditures, household members, employment, and debts, we calculate and analyze the following indicators:

First, the social dependency ratio.[7] In our calculation, the total dependency ratio is 1.65, which means that a sample driver has to support an average of 1.65 dependents, which is quite a heavy burden.

Second, the household income-expenditure ratio.[8] In this case, the household income-expenditure ratio is 1.79, indicating that the household income is greater than its expenditures. With a stable income, online ride-hailing drivers are capable of provide for their families.

Third, the asset-liability ratio.[9] The asset-liability ratio averaged 2.81 among our sample drivers. This indicates that they have certain degree of risk aversion and are able to settle down in cities.

Fourth, the proportion of online ride-hailing income to overall income. In our calculation, online rideshare income accounts for 26 percent of overall individual income. It is important part of individual income and reduces the burden of the drivers.

---

7 By reference to the "social dependency ratio" demographic, we establish the indicator of a "household dependency ratio," which is "(number of household members − number of household members employed)/number of household members employed." When this indicator is 0, all the household members are employed, indicating a light dependency burden. The greater the value, the heavier the dependency burden.

8 The household "income-expenditure ratio" is "monthly household total income divided by monthly household total expenditures." The greater the value, the greater capacity for savings a family has, and the smaller its burden.

9 The "asset-liability ratio" is the household assets divided by the household debt, the former including the property and vehicle(s) in the possession of a family, and the latter including housing mortgage(s), car loan(s), and private borrowings.

TABLE 4.1    Description of family burdens[a]

| Variable/Indicator | Mean | Standard deviation | Minimum | Maximum | Number of samples |
|---|---|---|---|---|---|
| Total dependency ratio | 1.65 | 1.31 | 0 | 7 | 29,820[b] |
| Income-expenditure ratio | 1.79 | 1.40 | 0.0484 | 38.75 | 30,623 |
| Asset-liability ratio | 2.81 | 2.88 | 0.076923 | 14 | 16,647 |
| Online ride-hailing income/ overall individual income | 0.26 | 0.25 | 0.000018 | 0.9997 | 23,734 |

Notes: a As for the "income-expenditure ratio," we have adopted a sorted list instead of specific values. This is because it was designed as a select range in the questionnaire, and significant deviations can occur if we calculate it using specific values. To some degree, the current method also reflects the household burden of the sample drivers.

b When we calculate the total dependency ratio, 767 sample households have no members employed and are treated as missing samples, while 84 households have more employed members than household members and are therefore regarded as invalid samples. Given such exclusions, we have 29,820 valid samples.

## 3    Characteristics of Part-Time Online Ride-Hailing Drivers

One of the most important characteristics of the sharing economy is the "part-time (odd-job) economy," as internet-based platforms create abundant job opportunities aimed at satisfying the market's need for products and services. As our statistical analysis shows, part-time online ride-hailing drivers come from all levels of society and display diversified employment characteristics. Car owners from all walks of life enroll in ride-hailing and car sharing in their spare time. Meanwhile, among part-time drivers, many are freelancers, flexible workers, self-employed laborers, and under-employed laborers, for whom ride-hailing income constitutes an important part of their regular income.

### 3.1    *Regular Jobs Held by Part-Time Drivers*

As previously mentioned, part-time drivers are from all walks of life and exhibit diversified characteristics in terms of their primary employment. Their regular jobs are associated with various work units, such as party and government offices, state-owned enterprises, foreign-funded enterprises, and being self-employed. The largest number comes from enterprises and public institutions/government offices, accounting for 30.81 percent of all part-time drivers, and they mainly work in conventional manufacturing sectors and traditional services.

# EMPLOYMENT AND WORK ON ONLINE RIDE-HAILING PLATFORMS 81

It must be specifically noted that 29.24 percent of these part-time drivers come from conventional capacity-reduction sectors, such as manufacturing, steel, and coal. A number of employees from such sectors serve as part-time drivers and gain an additional source of revenue in order to improve their living conditions.

TABLE 4.2　Regular jobs of part-time Didi drivers

| Indicator | Grouping | Samples | Proportion (percent) | Cumulative proportion (percent) |
|---|---|---|---|---|
| Current job | Enterprises and public institutions/government offices | 4,961 | 30.81 | 30.81 |
| | Owner (partner) of enterprises | 1,157 | 7.18 | 37.99 |
| | Odd jobs | 2,716 | 16.87 | 54.86 |
| | Individual business owner | 2,446 | 15.19 | 70.05 |
| | Self-employed/freelancer | 3,507 | 21.78 | 91.83 |
| | Others | 1,316 | 8.17 | 100.00 |
| | Total | 16,103 | 100.00 | |
| Type of work units* | Party and government offices/ public institutions | 1,001 | 9.86 | 9.86 |
| | State-owned, state-holding, and collectively-owned enterprises | 2,050 | 20.20 | 30.06 |
| | Foreign-funded enterprises Hong Kong-, Macao-, and Taiwan-funded enterprises | 883 | 8.70 | 38.76 |
| | Private enterprises | 4,140 | 40.79 | 79.55 |
| | Jobless/self-employed/ owner (partner) of enterprises | 876 | 8.63 | 88.18 |
| | Social organizations | 289 | 2.85 | 91.02 |
| | Others | 911 | 8.98 | 100.00 |
| | Total | 10,150 | 100.00 | |
| Current position | Ordinary staff/operators/ merchandisers/purchasing agents | 3,903 | 38.45 | 38.45 |
| | Professional and technical personnel/engineers | 1,988 | 19.59 | 58.04 |
| | Office and administrative staff | 830 | 8.18 | 66.22 |

TABLE 4.2 Regular jobs of part-time Didi drivers (*cont.*)

| Indicator | Grouping | Samples | Proportion (percent) | Cumulative proportion (percent) |
|---|---|---|---|---|
| | Low-level managers (business management specialists/business executives) | 1,215 | 11.97 | 78.19 |
| | Mid-level and senior managers | 848 | 8.35 | 86.54 |
| | Others | 1,366 | 13.46 | 100.00 |
| | Total | 10,150 | 100.00 | |
| Industry/ sector | Traditional manufacturing (e.g., textiles, machine manufacturing, chemical manufacturing, cement, aluminum, etc.) | 4,190 | 26.02 | 26.02 |
| | Steel- and coal-relevant sectors | 518 | 3.22 | 29.24 |
| | Traditional services (e.g., hoteling, retail sales, catering, etc.) | 2,664 | 16.54 | 45.78 |
| | Modern services (e.g., finance, intermediary agent, consultation, e-commerce, etc.) | 1,851 | 11.49 | 57.28 |
| | Transportation | 2,497 | 15.51 | 72.78 |
| | Health/education/public management organizations/ government agencies and organizations | 1,165 | 7.23 | 80.02 |
| | Agriculture and animal husbandry | 457 | 2.84 | 82.85 |
| | Others | 2,761 | 17.15 | 100.00 |
| | Total | 16,103 | 100.00 | |
| Contract with employer | No contract or agreement | 6,553 | 40.69 | 40.69 |
| | Short-term employment contract | 2,583 | 16.04 | 56.73 |
| | Fixed-term employment contract | 4,651 | 28.88 | 85.62 |
| | Labor service agreement | 1,746 | 10.84 | 96.46 |
| | Temporary work agreement | 570 | 3.54 | 100.00 |
| | Total | 16,103 | 100.00 | |

Note: "Type of work unit" and "current position" applies only to the first three types of samples included here, while "Others" refers to those with specific work units, i.e., "Enterprises and public institutions/government offices", "Owner (partner) of enterprises", "Odd jobs", and "Others."

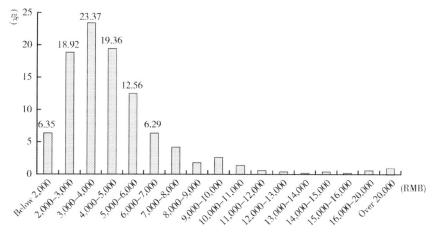

FIGURE 4.17   Part-time drivers' monthly income from regular jobs

### 3.2   *Part-Time Drivers' Income from Regular Jobs*

The regular jobs of part-time Didi drivers are typified by long working hours but relatively low wages. The largest proportion (23.37 percent) of part-time drivers make RMB 3,000 to RMB 4,000 per month in their regular jobs, while the average income from part-time drivers' regular jobs is RMB 4,705 per month. 48.64 percent of part-time drivers make less than RMB 4,000 per month from their regular jobs, which is relatively low. Over 80 percent of the part-time drivers work five to seven days per week. The largest proportion (42.59 percent) work eight hours a day, while 38.25 percent of part-time drivers work more than eight hours a day.

On average, part-time drivers work 5.29 days per week in their regular jobs, and the largest proportion of these (35.02 percent) work five days per week.

In terms of working hours, part-time drivers work 8.42 hours a day on average, with the largest proportion (42.59 percent) of part-time drivers working eight hours a day. In general, part-time drivers work long hours in their regular jobs.

### 3.3   *Social Security for Part-Time Didi Drivers*

Nearly half of the part-time drivers surveyed have been provided with the "five social insurances and one Housing Provident Fund" by their regular employers, including: employee pension insurance (58.04 percent), employee medical insurance (62.16 percent), unemployment insurance (48.38 percent), employment injury insurance (53.76 percent), and maternity insurance (41.07 percent).

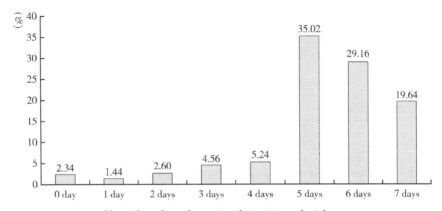

FIGURE 4.18  Weekly working days of part-time drivers in regular jobs

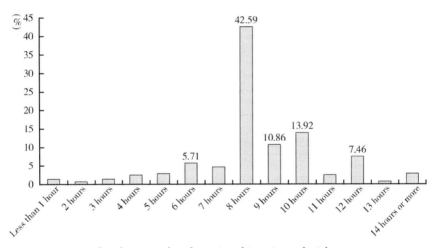

FIGURE 4.19  Working hours per day of part-time drivers in regular jobs

Yet relatively few part-time drivers are entitled to the Housing Provident Fund. According to our calculations, only 34.73 percent of part-time drivers are provided with a Housing Provident Fund by their work units.

Besides, only a small proportion of the part-time drivers are provided with commercial insurances. According to our statistics, approximately two-thirds of all part-time drivers are not provided with either commercial endowment insurance (66.57 percent) or commercial medical insurance (63.23 percent).

TABLE 4.3  Social security provided by regular employers

| Social security | Grouping | Samples | Proportion (percent) | Cumulative proportion (percent) |
|---|---|---|---|---|
| Employee pension insurance | Yes | 9,346 | 58.04 | 58.04 |
| | No | 5,974 | 37.10 | 95.14 |
| | Uncertain | 783 | 4.86 | 100.00 |
| | Total | 16,103 | 100.00 | |
| Employee medical insurance | Yes | 10,010 | 62.16 | 62.16 |
| | No | 5,355 | 33.25 | 95.42 |
| | Uncertain | 738 | 4.58 | 100.00 |
| | Total | 16,103 | 100.00 | |
| Unemployment insurance | Yes | 7,791 | 48.38 | 48.38 |
| | No | 7,060 | 43.84 | 92.23 |
| | Uncertain | 1,252 | 7.77 | 100.00 |
| | Total | 16,103 | 100.00 | |
| Employment injury insurance | Yes | 8,657 | 53.76 | 53.76 |
| | No | 6,304 | 39.15 | 92.91 |
| | Uncertain | 1,142 | 7.09 | 100.00 |
| | Total | 16,103 | 100.00 | |
| Maternity insurance | Yes | 6,613 | 41.07 | 41.07 |
| | No | 7,765 | 48.22 | 89.29 |
| | Uncertain | 1,725 | 10.71 | 100.00 |
| | Total | 16,103 | 100.00 | |

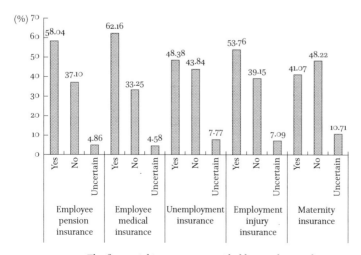

FIGURE 4.20  The five social insurances provided by regular employers

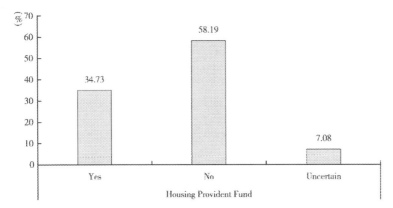

FIGURE 4.21   Housing provident fund provided by regular employers

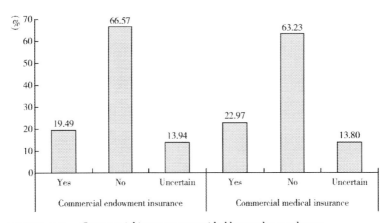

FIGURE 4.22   Commercial insurances provided by regular employers

## 4   Characteristics of Full-Time Online Ride-Hailing Drivers

With the rapid development of the sharing economy, when laborers are capable of obtaining stable income from various internet-based platforms, some of them have come to regard their job under the sharing economy as their major source of income, even considering it their "profession." Statistics gathered on all online ride-hailing drivers on the Didi platform show that while some are part-time drivers looking to increase their income, others work as full-time rideshare drivers.

EMPLOYMENT AND WORK ON ONLINE RIDE-HAILING PLATFORMS

## 4.1    *Characteristics of Full-Time Drivers' Previous Jobs*

Most full-time drivers used to work in traditional manufacturing and services. They have now chosen to work as full-time rideshare drivers specifically because the new job provides a stable income, more flexible working hours, and greater autonomy and freedom.

These full-time drivers came from all walks of life, such as former employees of enterprises and public institutions/government offices, individual business owners, the self-employed, and ex-soldiers. This model of employment has, to some degree, solved the unemployment problem for some people. As we find, 6.31 percent of current full-time drivers were unemployed until they become ride-hailing drivers. Before they became ride-hailing drivers, most (now) full-time drivers took odd jobs, ran individual businesses, or were self-employed or working as freelancers. Even if some belonged to work units, most of them worked in private enterprises. In terms of positions, most of them worked as ordinary staff, operators, merchandisers, or purchasing agents. Most full-time drivers used to work in traditional manufacturing and services.

TABLE 4.4    Previous jobs of full-time Didi drivers

| Indicator | Grouping | Samples | Proportion (percent) | Cumulative proportion (percent) |
|---|---|---|---|---|
| Previous job | Enterprises and public institutions/government offices | 1,396 | 14.94 | 14.94 |
|  | Owner/Partner of enterprises | 390 | 4.17 | 19.11 |
|  | Odd jobs | 2,418 | 25.87 | 44.99 |
|  | Individual business owner | 1,421 | 15.21 | 60.19 |
|  | Self-employed/freelancer | 1,089 | 11.65 | 71.85 |
|  | Taxi driver | 636 | 6.81 | 78.65 |
|  | Illegal taxi driver | 368 | 3.94 | 82.59 |
|  | Jobless | 590 | 6.31 | 88.90 |
|  | Soldier | 105 | 1.12 | 90.03 |
|  | Retired | 29 | 0.31 | 90.34 |
|  | Others | 903 | 9.66 | 100.00 |
|  | Total | 9,345 | 100.00 |  |

TABLE 4.4    Previous jobs of full-time Didi drivers (*cont.*)

| Indicator | Grouping | Samples | Proportion (percent) | Cumulative proportion (percent) |
|---|---|---|---|---|
| Type of former work units | Party and government offices/ public institutions | 190 | 7.07 | 7.07 |
| | State-owned, state-held, and collectively-owned enterprises | 467 | 17.37 | 24.43 |
| | Foreign-funded enterprises Hong Kong-, Macao-, and Taiwan-funded enterprises | 254 | 9.45 | 33.88 |
| | Private enterprises | 1,288 | 47.90 | 81.78 |
| | Jobless/self-employed/ owner (partner) of enterprises | 220 | 8.18 | 89.96 |
| | Social organizations | 47 | 1.75 | 91.71 |
| | Others | 223 | 8.29 | 100.00 |
| | Total | 2,689 | 100.00 | |
| Previous position | Ordinary staff/operators/ merchandisers/purchasing agents | 818 | 30.42 | 30.42 |
| | Professional and technical personnel/engineers | 392 | 14.58 | 45.00 |
| | Office and administrative staff | 251 | 9.33 | 54.33 |
| | Low-level managers (business management specialists/ business executives) | 444 | 16.51 | 70.84 |
| | Mid-level and senior managers | 382 | 14.21 | 85.05 |
| | Others | 402 | 14.95 | 100.00 |
| | Total | 2,689 | 100.00 | |

# EMPLOYMENT AND WORK ON ONLINE RIDE-HAILING PLATFORMS

TABLE 4.4    Previous jobs of full-time Didi drivers (*cont.*)

| Indicator | Grouping | Samples | Proportion (percent) | Cumulative proportion (percent) |
|---|---|---|---|---|
| Industry/sector | Traditional manufacturing (e.g., textile, machine manufacturing, chemical manufacturing, cement, aluminum, etc.) | 1,825 | 23.96 | 23.96 |
| | Steel- and coal-relevant sectors | 208 | 2.73 | 26.96 |
| | Traditional services (e.g., hoteling, retail sales, catering, etc.) | 1,738 | 22.82 | 49.51 |
| | Modern services (e.g., finance, intermediary agent, consultation, e-commerce, etc.) | 684 | 8.98 | 58.49 |
| | Transportation | 1,463 | 19.21 | 77.69 |
| | Health/education/public management organizations/ government agencies and organizations | 185 | 2.43 | 80.12 |
| | Agriculture and animal husbandry | 337 | 4.42 | 84.55 |
| | Others | 1,177 | 15.45 | 100.00 |
| | Total | 7,617 | 100.00 | |
| Length of unemployment | 0 months | 2,951 | 31.58 | 31.58 |
| | 1–3 months | 3,054 | 32.68 | 64.26 |
| | 3–6 months | 1,153 | 12.34 | 76.60 |
| | 6–9 months | 543 | 5.81 | 82.41 |
| | 9–12 months | 484 | 5.18 | 87.59 |
| | 1–2 years | 547 | 5.85 | 93.44 |
| | Over 2 years | 613 | 6.56 | 100.00 |
| | Total | 9,345 | 100.00 | |

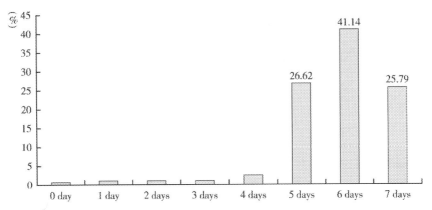

FIGURE 4.23   Previous jobs of full-time Didi drivers: working days per week

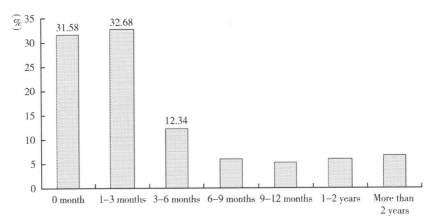

FIGURE 4.24   Jobless period before becoming full-time Didi drivers

Before they became full-time Didi drivers, the largest proportion (41.14 percent) had to work six days a week, with long working hours coupled with relatively little freedom. Before they turned to online ride-hailing, the largest proportion either made between RMB 3,000 and RMB 4,000 (21.81 percent) or RMB 4,000 and RMB 5,000 (20.23 percent) per month. The largest proportion (38.13 percent) worked up to eight hours a day, while 52.37 percent of them worked eight hours or more a day. Generally speaking, their previous jobs were characterized by high working intensity but relatively low wages. Now, as full-time Didi drivers, they are entitled to more flexible working hours along with greater autonomy and freedom.

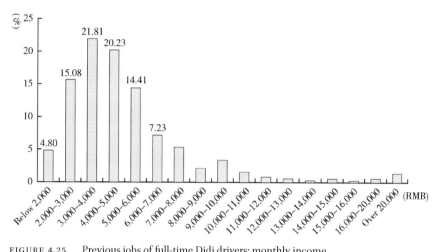

FIGURE 4.25   Previous jobs of full-time Didi drivers: monthly income

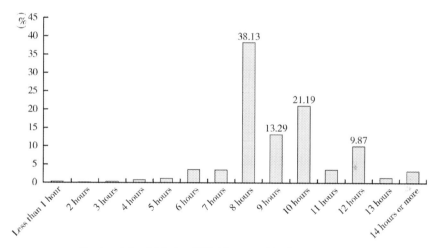

FIGURE 4.26   Previous jobs of full-time Didi drivers: working hours

Before they became full-time Didi drivers, the largest proportion (41.14 percent) had to work six days a week. By offering job opportunities and alternative sources of income, the online ride-hailing platform has more or less solved long-term unemployment for a large amount of people. In fact, before they became full-time Didi drivers, the largest proportion (32.68 percent) had been unemployed for one to three months.

Before they turned to online ride-hailing, the largest proportion of workers (21.81 percent) made between RMB 3,000 and RMB 4,000 per month, and the largest proportion (38.13 percent) had to work eight hours a day on average.

### 4.2 *Social Security for Full-Time Didi Drivers*

Compared with employees' pension insurance and employees' medical insurance, a larger proportion of full-time Didi drivers have enrolled in the urban residents' basic medical insurance/new rural cooperative medical system and/ or the endowment insurance for urban residents/new rural social pension insurance.

TABLE 4.5    Full-time Didi drivers' participation in commercial insurances

| Commercial insurance | Grouping | Samples | Proportion (percent) | Cumulative proportion (percent) |
|---|---|---|---|---|
| Commercial medical insurance | Yes | 1,714 | 18.34 | 18.34 |
| | No | 6,341 | 67.85 | 86.20 |
| | Uncertain | 1,290 | 13.80 | 100.00 |
| | Total | 9,345 | 100.00 | |
| Commercial pension insurance | Yes | 1,164 | 12.46 | 12.46 |
| | No | 6,815 | 72.93 | 85.38 |
| | Uncertain | 1,366 | 14.62 | 100.00 |
| | Total | 9,345 | 100.00 | |

TABLE 4.6(A)    Full-time Didi drivers' participation in social security

| Social security | Grouping | Samples | Proportion (percent) | Cumulative proportion (percent) |
|---|---|---|---|---|
| Employee's pension insurance | Yes | 2,394 | 25.62 | 25.62 |
| | No | 5,997 | 64.17 | 89.79 |
| | Uncertain | 954 | 10.21 | 100.00 |
| | Total | 9,345 | 100.00 | |
| Employee's medical insurance | Yes | 2,479 | 26.53 | 26.53 |
| | No | 5,919 | 63.34 | 89.87 |
| | Uncertain | 947 | 10.13 | 100.00 |
| | Total | 9,345 | 100.00 | |

EMPLOYMENT AND WORK ON ONLINE RIDE-HAILING PLATFORMS 93

TABLE 4.6(B)   Full-time Didi drivers' participation in social security

| Social security | Grouping | Samples | Proportion (percent) | Cumulative proportion (percent) |
|---|---|---|---|---|
| Urban residents' basic medical insurance/new rural cooperative medical system | Yes | 3,491 | 37.36 | 37.36 |
| | No | 4,719 | 50.50 | 87.85 |
| | Uncertain | 1,135 | 12.15 | 100.00 |
| | Total | 9,345 | 100.00 | |
| Endowment insurance for urban residents/new rural social pension insurance | Yes | 4,904 | 52.48 | 52.48 |
| | No | 3,418 | 36.58 | 89.05 |
| | Uncertain | 1,023 | 10.95 | 100.00 |
| | Total | 9,345 | 100.00 | |

As our statistics suggest, around two-thirds of all full-time drivers have not participated or do not enroll in an employees' pension insurance (64.17 percent) or employees' medical insurance (63.34 percent), but a smaller proportion of them have taken part in commercial insurances. Over two-thirds of all full-time drivers have not enrolled in commercial medical insurance (67.85 percent) or commercial pension insurance (72.93 percent).

Meanwhile, a larger proportion of full-time Didi drivers have enrolled in either the urban residents' basic medical insurance/new rural cooperative medical system (37.36 percent) or the endowment insurance for urban residents/new rural social pension insurance (52.48 percent).

## 5      Job Characteristics of Didi Drivers

### 5.1     *Characteristics of the Current Job*

Didi drivers are a fairly stable group, consisting mainly of drivers with at least one year of driving experience. They have a wealth of both driving and working experiences behind them, with 36.87 percent (the largest proportion of all groups) of Didi drivers having six to ten years of driving experience and 30.78 percent (the largest proportion of all groups) of Didi drivers having a working experience of eleven years before they turned to online ride-hailing. Over 50 percent of Didi drivers have worked for at least ten years.

TABLE 4.7    Job characteristics of sample Didi drivers

| Indicator | Grouping | Samples | Proportion (percent) | Cumulative proportion (percent) |
|---|---|---|---|---|
| Previous work experience | 1–5 years | 4,652 | 15.17 | 15.17 |
| | 6–10 years | 10,010 | 32.63 | 47.80 |
| | Over 10 years | 16,009 | 52.20 | 100.00 |
| | Total | 30,671 | 100.00 | |
| Driving experience | Less than 3 years | 562 | 2.04 | 2.04 |
| | 3–5 years | 7,158 | 25.93 | 27.97 |
| | 6–10 years | 10,177 | 36.87 | 64.85 |
| | Over 10 years | 9,702 | 35.13 | 100.00 |
| | Total | 27,599 | 100.00 | |
| Source of vehicles | Private cars bought (from 4S stores) in cash | 16,163 | 52.70 | 52.70 |
| | Private cars bought (from 4S stores) by installment | 11,614 | 37.87 | 90.56 |
| | Lease purchase | 975 | 3.18 | 93.74 |
| | Rented | 633 | 2.06 | 95.81 |
| | Others | 1,286 | 4.19 | 100.00 |
| | Total | 30,671 | 100.00 | |
| Age of cars | 0–3 years | 16,734 | 61.33 | 61.33 |
| | 3–5 years | 5,678 | 20.81 | 82.15 |
| | 5–8 years | 4,339 | 15.90 | 98.05 |
| | Over 8 years | 532 | 1.95 | 100.00 |
| | Total | 27,283 | 100.00 | |
| As Didi drivers | Less than 1 year | 5,726 | 20.73 | 20.73 |
| | 1–2 years | 14,196 | 51.39 | 72.11 |
| | 2–3 years | 7,625 | 27.60 | 99.71 |
| | Over 3 years | 79 | 0.29 | 100.00 |
| | Total | 27,626 | 100.00 | |

Note: The samples herein are smaller than those of the questionnaire samples. This is because the above variables (indicators) are backend statistics. Yet the backend data of all 3,045 questionnaire samples is not available on the platform, because the drivers have either changed their phone numbers or been banned from service.

EMPLOYMENT AND WORK ON ONLINE RIDE-HAILING PLATFORMS 95

TABLE 4.8    Average monthly ride orders accepted by Didi drivers

| Variable | Drivers | Mean | Standard deviation | Samples |
|---|---|---|---|---|
| Average monthly orders | Overall | 145 | 151.11 | 27,581 |
| | Full-time | 262 | 178.76 | 8,122 |
| | Part-time | 100 | 105.70 | 14,655 |

In terms of their experiences with Didi and vehicle conditions, most drivers joined the platform more than a year prior to this survey, a figure which remains relatively stable. Their cars are generally new and bought through various channels, as the threshold for purchasing a new one is rather low. More than half of Didi drivers have bought their own car with cash in order to join the Didi platform, and most of their cars are less than three years old.

There are various channels for drivers to buy new cars, as the barrier for entry to work is low. 37.87 percent of Didi drivers have bought a private car (from Automobile Sales Serviceshops or 4S stores) by installment or borrowing. The threshold of online ride-hailing is fairly low, and many drivers have obtained the means of production through different channels and, subsequently, joined the profession.

## 5.2    *Characteristics of Work Behavior*[10]

In this section, we will describe Didi drivers' work behavior in light of the number of ride orders they accept, their online hours, driving hours, mileage, income, and number of complaints.

### 5.2.1    Average Monthly Ride Orders Accepted

Generally, full-time drivers take more orders than part-time drivers, but part-time drivers are more flexible. After completing their regular jobs, part-time Didi drivers may accept ride orders at their convenience, which reflects the flexibility of hailing a ride online—it is free from the restrictions typically imposed by time, profession, and location. Moreover, the drivers are free from the platform in terms of the time and place of their work. Full-time Didi drivers, on the other hand, regard online ride-hailing as their entire profession and work hard to increase their income through accepting ride orders exclusively.

According to statistics, an online ride-hailing driver takes 145 orders on average per month. Specifically, a full-time driver takes 262 orders per month, and a part-time driver takes 100 orders per month.

---

10    The samples include full-time, part-time, and former Didi drivers.

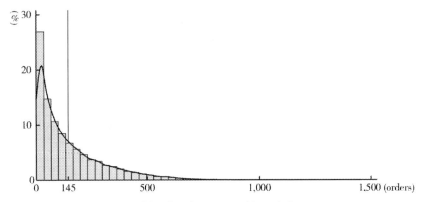

FIGURE 4.27    Average monthly ride orders accepted by Didi drivers

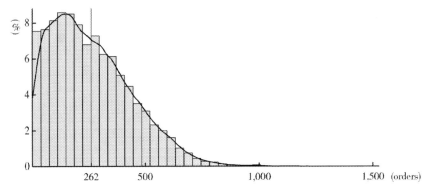

FIGURE 4.28 (A)    Average monthly ride orders accepted by full-time Didi drivers

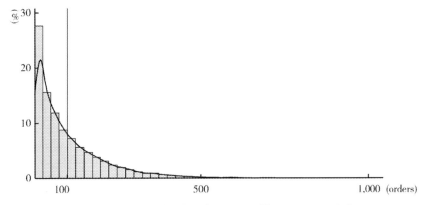

FIGURE 4.28 (B)    Average monthly ride orders accepted by part-time Didi drivers

### 5.2.2 Average Monthly Driving Hours

The hours served working by part-time drivers on the Didi platform reflects their great flexibility and degree of freedom. On average, Didi drivers serve 35.70 hours per month on the platform. Specifically, part-time drivers serve 24 hours per month, and full-time drivers serve 66 hours per month.

TABLE 4.9  Average monthly driving hours of Didi drivers

| Variable | Drivers | Mean | Standard deviation | Minimum | Maximum | Samples |
|---|---|---|---|---|---|---|
| Average Monthly Driving Hours | Overall | 35.70 | 37.76 | 0 | 266.76 | 27,581 |
|  | Full-time | 66 | 44.80 | 0 | 267 | 8,122 |
|  | Part-time | 24 | 24.97 | 0 | 214 | 14,655 |

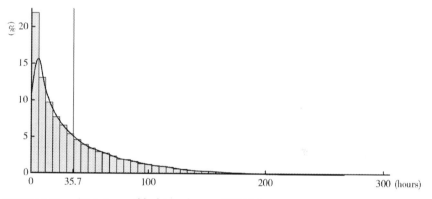

FIGURE 4.29  Average monthly driving hours of Didi drivers

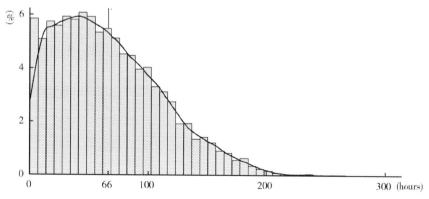

FIGURE 4.30 (A)  Average monthly driving hours of full-time Didi drivers

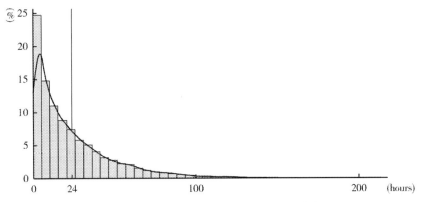

FIGURE 4.30 (B)   Average monthly driving hours of part-time Didi drivers

TABLE 4.10   Average monthly income of Didi drivers

| Variable | Drivers | Mean | Standard deviation | Minimum | Maximum | Samples |
|---|---|---|---|---|---|---|
| Average monthly income | Overall | 2,395.28 | 2,887.23 | 0 | 27,352.33 | 27,568 |
| | Full-time | 4,641 | 3,659.62 | 3.51 | 27,352 | 8,118 |
| | Part-time | 1,495 | 1,755.53 | 0 | 22,139 | 14,649 |

### 5.2.3   Average Monthly Income

The Didi platform not only guarantees stable and sustainable income for its full-time drivers, but also enables part-time drivers to make good use of their flexible time and increase their income.

Online ridesharing provides a stable source of income. As a result of their more intense workload, full-time Didi drivers obtain a correspondingly higher income from online ride-hailing. On the other hand, part-time Didi drivers can make good use of their flexible time while still increasing their income. On average, a Didi driver makes RMB 2,395.28 per month from online ride-hailing, with a maximum of RMB 27,352.33 per month. A full-time Didi driver makes RMB 4,641 per month from online ride-hailing, with a maximum of RMB 27,352 per month, and a part-time Didi driver makes RMB 1,495 per month from online ride-hailing, with a maximum of RMB 22,139 per month.

The above are representative statistics of sample drivers nationwide. If we classify all cities considered into different groups, drivers in first-tier cities and

EMPLOYMENT AND WORK ON ONLINE RIDE-HAILING PLATFORMS 99

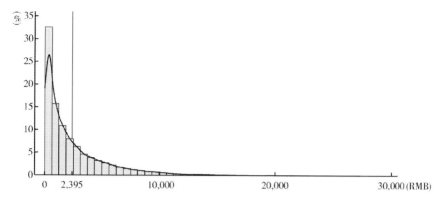

FIGURE 4.31    Average monthly income of Didi drivers

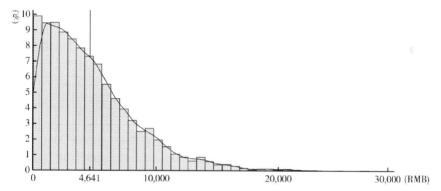

FIGURE 4.32 (A)    Average monthly income of full-time Didi drivers

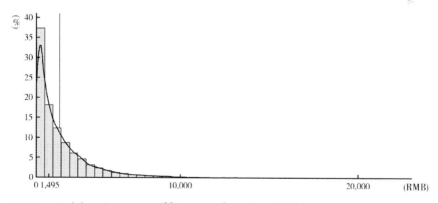

FIGURE 4.32 (B)    Average monthly income of part-time Didi drivers

TABLE 4.11   Average monthly income of Didi drivers (by type of city)

| Type of cities | Full-time drivers | Part-time drivers | Average monthly income |
| --- | --- | --- | --- |
| First-tier cities | 7,328.29 | 2,475.3 | 4,690.13 |
| New first-tier cities | 4,531.05 | 1,552.89 | 2,636.76 |
| Second-tier cities | 3,930.73 | 1,396.37 | 2,277.57 |
| Others | 2,429.96 | 917.47 | 1,332.03 |

new first-tier cities[11] obviously earn much more than those in other cities. In a first-tier city, a full-time Didi driver makes RMB 7,328.29 per month on average, and a part-time Didi driver makes RMB 2,475.3 per month. In a new first-tier city, a full-time Didi driver makes RMB 4,531.05 per month on average, and a part-time Didi driver makes RMB 1,552.89 per month.

## 6    Policy Suggestions

In this chapter, we analyzed both group and job characteristics shared by online ride-hailing drivers. As a result of the field's explosive growth over the past few years, the sharing economy has developed into a brand new force. In 2016, China became the first country to legalize online ridesharing. Yet it is still inadequate in terms of the policies, laws, and regulations concerning the administration and regulation of the online ride-hailing market, especially insofar as the institutional construction concerning the work and employment of online ride-hailing drivers. Accordingly, we put forward the following policy suggestions.

---

11    On May 25, 2017, the Institute for New First-Tier Cities under the China Business Network released its classifications of Chinese cities at a conference titled "The Rising Summit: Commercial Charm Rankings of Chinese Cities 2017." Those considered first-tier cities are Beijing, Shanghai, Guangzhou, and Shenzhen. The 15 new first-tier cities are: Chengdu, Hangzhou, Wuhan, Chongqing, Nanjing, Tianjin, Suzhou, Xi'an, Changsha, Shenyang, Qingdao, Zhengzhou, Dalian, Dongguan, and Ningbo. The 30 second-tier cities include Xiamen, Fuzhou, Wuxi, Hefei, etc. The rest are classified as "Other Cities." In line with such classifications, we have also classified the cities under study into these four types.

First of all, we must encourage and guide the development of the online ride-hailing market and improve both the institutions themselves and the measures for market access and regulation.

Since August 2016, several successive new policies have been introduced in different parts of China. Local governments and regulators have also introduced new, corresponding market access and regulative policies in line with local market characteristics. In some areas, such policies have been implemented for almost a full year already. Over the past year, different regions have varied in their enforcement of new policies concerning online ridesharing, and it has been unclear to what extent changes may be implemented. Such elements have had a considerable influence on both the online ride-hailing market and online rideshare drivers. Strict market access and regulatory institutions and measures are conducive to the establishment of a normative market, but we must focus on the sharing economy as an innovative market when formulating policies, laws, and regulations. As an innovative market that facilitates travel, the online rideshare market must lower its market access threshold while still ensuring traffic safety.

Secondly, we must fully bring into play the sharing economy's role in boosting employment and, in doing so, attach further importance to its role in generating income for laborers.

Due to recent technological innovations, the sharing economy provides laborers with new opportunities for obtaining extra income. In our research, we surveyed how drivers view online ride-hailing, finding that 69.08 percent of the sample drivers think it brings in extra income. In other words, nearly 70 percent of drivers perceive online ride-hailing as a new source of income. From this, it follows that online ride-hailing plays a significant role in creating job opportunities and increasing income. Given that part-time Didi drivers come from all walks of life, online ride-hailing is of profound significance for those with low and unstable income from their regular jobs. Unlike part-time Didi drivers, full-time Didi drivers are more dependent on the online rideshare market, which is the major source of their income. When the sharing economy develops from the gig economy, it becomes obvious that the sharing economy is now particularly important in creating new, stable sources of income.

Thirdly, we must positively direct further changes to the concept of employment and fully recognize the current condition and role of the sharing economy in the labor market.

Following the rapid development of internet technology, great changes have taken place to traditional concepts and modes of employment. As we see it, in addition to the employment relationship, participation in the sharing economy is also an important mode of employment. With the increased number of laborers engaging in the sharing economy, it is necessary to change the traditional concepts of employment and fully recognize the current condition and role of the sharing economy in the labor market. This is extremely important for boosting the development of the sharing economy and promoting both employment quantity and quality. We believe that guiding future changes to the concept of employment will be necessary for adjusting future policies. Given that the sharing economy is an important field of employment for the overall labor market, our policies must more actively guide those laborers trapped in underemployment or frictional unemployment situations, so as to constantly increase the participation rate in our labor market and improve overall employment quality.

Fourthly, we must revise existing labor laws and regulations and redefine those rules and institutions that are related to the sharing economy.

At present, the labor laws of every country are grounded on the employment relationship, emphasizing the rights and obligations of both the employer and employee. Under the sharing economy, however, fundamental changes have taken place amongst the participants of the labor market, the modes of work, the methods of payment, and how work processes are controlled. An analysis of the job characteristics of Didi drivers reveals that online rideshare drivers are quite different from people working in traditional employment relationship. The fundamental difference lies in the nature of their labor. Labor performed by an employee is what we call paid labor. In other words, they earn remuneration for the work they do. By contrast, the labor provided by online rideshare drivers is based on the completion of an individual assignment. Their income depends on the completion of the assignments. Now that we have established this fundamental difference, it is necessary to reevaluate the rules, rights, and duties of work.

Finally, we must reform and improve the country's existing social security policy and provide laborers with a basic guarantee for their entry into and withdrawal from the labor market.

For laborers employed by the sharing economy, China's existing social security policy has not been able to provide a basic guarantee for their entry into and withdrawal from the labor market. We deem it necessary to adjust and reform China's social security policy as soon as possible and to incorporate sharing-economy laborers into our broader social security system. We must not only guarantee the stability and sustainability of their income after they have entered the labor market, but also ensure a base level of social security for them when they withdraw from the labor market.

## Acknowledgements

This chapter is the end result of a major scientific research project spearheaded by the "Digital Technology Revolution and the Future of the Work World," a key program of the Scientific Research Fund of Renmin University of China.

## Author Biographies

Wu Qingjun is an associate professor at the School of Labor and Human Resources and the chairperson of the Labor Relations Department, Renmin University of China. His academic interests include corporate labor relations management, collective conference and negotiation, and trade unions.

Yang Weiguo is a professor, Ph.D. supervisor, and the Dean of the School of Labor and Human Resources, Renmin University of China. His academic interests include theories and policies of labor economics, the auditing of strategic human resources, and strategic human resource management.

Wang Qi and Chen Xiaofei are Ph.D. candidates at the School of Labor and Human Resources, Renmin University of China.

## References

Boston Consulting Group (BCG), *Restructuring Employment in the Internet Age*, 2015, http://www.bcg.com.cn/cn/newsandpublications/publications/reports/report 20150812001.html.

China Internet Network Information Center, *Report on the Development of the Online Ride-Hailing Market* (2015), http://www.cnnic.net.cn/hlwfzyj/hlwxzbg/ydhlwbg /201601/t20160104_53177.htm.

Dokko, Jane, Megan Munford, and Diane Whitmore Schanzenbach, "Workers and the Online Gig Economy," 2015, working paper, http.//www.hamiltonproject.org/assets /files/workers_and_the_online_gig_economy.pdf.

Hall, Jonathan, and Alan Krueger, "An Analysis of the Labor Market for Uber's Driver-Partners in the United States," working paper, https://dataspace.princeton .edu/jspui/bitstream/88435/dspo10z708z67d/5/587.pdf.

Harris, Seth D. and Alan B. Krueger, "A Proposal for Modernizing Labor Laws for Twenty-First-Century Work: The 'Independent Worker'," 2015, working paper,

http://www.hamiltonproject.org/papers/modernizing_labor_laws_for_twenty_first_century_work_independent_worker/.

iResearch, *"Research Report on the Service Market of China's Online Ride-Hailing (2016),"* 2016, http://www.199it.com/archives/452810.html.

JPMorgan Chase & Co. Institute, "Paychecks, Paydays, and the Online Platform Economy," 2016, https://www.jpmorganchase.com/corporate/institute/report-paychecks-paydays-and-the-online-platform-economy.htm.

Kennedy, Joseph V. "Three Paths to Update Labor Law for the Gig Economy," 2016, working paper, http://www2.itif.org/2016-labor-law-gig-economy.pdf?_ga=1.18547377.946916969.1465339453.

Meeker, Mary, *Internet Trends 2016—CODE Conference*, 2016, http://tech.qq.com/a/20160602/001331.htm#p=1.

Occhiuto, Nicholas, "Investing in Independent Contract Work: The Significance of Schedule Control for Taxi Drivers," *Work and Occupations* 44 (2017): 268–295.

State Information Center (SIC) Research Center of Sharing Economy and The Internet Society of China (ISC) Sharing Economy Working Committee, *Report on the Development of China's Sharing Economy* (2017), http://www.sic.gov.cn/News/250/7737.htm.

State Information Center (SIC) Department of Informatization and Industry Development, *Report on the Development of the Global Information Society* (2016), http://www.sic.gov.cn/News/250/6354.htm.

CHAPTER 5

# The Role of Platform-Based Companies in Creating Employment Opportunities for Laid-Off Workers from Overcapacity Industries: a Case Study of the Didi Chuxing Platform

*Zhang Chenggang*

## 1 Introduction

Over the past five years, human society has entered the mobile internet era, and there has been a drastic decrease in market transaction costs. Meanwhile, boosted by new technologies, new forms of employment, and new models of business, the traditional concept of "informal employment" has been endowed with a new connotation: while it used to refer to work that was low-skill, low-paid, and shunned, it now often refers to jobs that are high-skilled, well-paying, and sought after.[1]

In this process, employment models formed by using platforms as an alternative market or enterprises to organize labor factors have emerged. Such models are what we call platform-based models of employment.[2] This model of employment is characterized by a flexible "employment" relationship, fragmented work, and a de-organization of working arrangements.[3] Platform-based companies are quite different from more traditional forms of employment in that in the latter, it is the employer who organizes production and the working hours and locations where work takes place are relatively fixed. According

---

1 Zhang Chenggang 张成刚, "Jiuye fazhan de weilai qushi xin jiuye xingyai de gainian ji yingxiang fenxin 就业发展的未来趋势，新就业形态的概念及影响分析 [The Future Trend of Employment Development: The Concept and Influence of New Forms of Employment]," *Human Resource Development of China* 19 (2016):86–91.

2 The term "employment" literally refers to the act of employing or state of being employed. In this context, employment is a model of work, which has nothing to do with the employment relationship or whether there an employment relationship exists.

3 Tang Kuang, Li Yanjun, and Xu Jingyun 唐镢、李彦君、徐景昀, "Gongxiang jingji qiye yonggong guanli yu laodonghetongfa zhidu chuanxin 共享经济企业用工管理与〈劳动合同法〉制度创新 [Employment Management of Sharing Economy Enterprises and the Institutional Innovation of the *Labor Contract Law*]," *China Labor* 14 (2016):41–52.

---

© KONINKLIJKE BRILL NV, LEIDEN, 2020 | DOI:10.1163/9789004435803_006

to the International Labor Organization,[4] the most profound influence on the future work world will be the connection between the demand side and the supply side of materials and services—a temporary business relation based on internet technology that no longer exists when the delivery of the designated product or service is completed.

Thanks to the rapid development of the new economy in the country, China is leading the world in platform-based companies in terms of the extent of its development, degree of innovation, and range of coverage. According to the *Report on the Development of China's Sharing Economy* (2017), "approximately 5.85 million people were employed on the sharing-economy platforms in 2016, up by 0.85 million from the previous year."[5] By the end of 2016, 17.509 million drivers had recived payment on the Didi platform.[6] The development of platform-based companies has greatly improved the efficiency of matching the supply of and demand for informal laborers on the labor market in Chinese cities.

Didi Chuxing is representative of China's platform-based companies. Because of its flexibility and the low threshold to join, the Didi Chuxing platform has become a major choice for the reemployment of those employees who have been laid off or affected by shutdowns in areas of industry that are at overcapacity. A considerable proportion of the Didi platform drivers are from these overcapacity industries. According to a report by the Didi Policy Research Institute (2016), by the end of May 2016, Didi Chuxing had provided 3.886 million job opportunities (including those provided by Didi Express/Premier and Designated Driving Service) for 17 key reduced-capacity provinces, accounting for 7.8 percent of the tertiary-industry employment in these provinces. Specifically, 1.231 million of the above-mentioned Didi drivers had been unemployed before joining the platform, 1.019 million came from the overcapacity industries, and 179,000 were army veterans.

The Chinese government has noticed the rapid development of the Didi Chuxing platform throughout the country and noted its huge potential for the reemployment of urban laid-off workers and employees in overcapacity industries. In December 2016, the Chinese Ministry of Human Resources and Social Security jointly issued the *Notice on Supporting Employment in the Northeast and Other Areas with Employment Difficulties*. The *Notice* proposed a

---

4   ILO, "The Future of Work Centenary Initiative," 2015.

5   State Information Center (SIC) Research Center of Sharing Economy, 2017.

6   Cheng Wei 程维, "Erlingyiqi nian jiuye yuanzhu xianchang tuijinhui jianghua 2017 年就业援助月现场推进会讲话 [Speech at the Site Promotion Meeting for the Employment Assistance Month of 2017]," December 2016.

THE ROLE OF PLATFORM-BASED COMPANIES

special support program in the online ride hailing sector and encouraged Didi and other similar sharing-economy enterprises to help reemploy the laid-off employees and employees affected by shutdowns. The *Notice* intended to carry out a pilot project of this special support program in Hebei, Shanxi, Liaoning, Jilin, and Heilongjiang from December 2016 to June 2017, which would help reemploy the laid-off employees and employees from enterprises that had shut down in these provinces who were willing to join the Didi platform. In 2016, 170,000 workers in the above-mentioned five provinces were laid off. Many more workers suffered from underemployment or a decrease in income due to the capacity reduction and poor industry performance.

## 2 Difficulties in Finding Employment Opportunities for Laid-Off Workers from Overcapacity Industries

For workers whose jobs are threatened by the country's efforts to reduce overcapacity, the government's overall objective is to "either reassign [them] to a different position or find them work in another profession." To that end, the government has called on corporations to offer alternatives to their own affected employees, including "entrepreneurship opportunities for those reassigned to other positions," "early retirement," and "employment guarantee." Surveys have shown that, when faced with redundant staff, 83 percent of enterprises choose to find alternatives opportunities for the affected employees from within the company, rather than laying them off or looking for opportunities for them from outside of the company.[7] However, these measures to place those employees from overcapacity enterprises have drawbacks.

First of all, the internal "digestion" of the affected employees puts enormous burden on these enterprises. On the one hand, reducing capacity involves huge numbers of employees, which is a significant pressure on the internal "digestion" of employees. If enterprises have to bear the cost of internal diversions, this is bound to impede their further transformation and upgrading. On the other hand, in the long run, in order to continue to grow, an enterprise has to allow the old to give place to the new and optimize the age structure of its workforce. The current placement measures, however, do not appear to serve these ends.

---

7   Li Xiaoman 李晓曼, "Huajie channenguosheng zhong de shou yingxiang zhigong guimo xianzhuang yu anzhi duice 化解产能过剩中的受影响职工：规模、现状与安置对策 [Workers Affected by Capacity Reduction: Number, Condition, and Placement Measures]," *Human Resource Development of China* 6 (2017): 18–24.

Secondly, with their relatively high thresholds for entry, innovation and entrepreneurship are unable to place the large number of workers affected by capacity reduction. It is true that the government and enterprises have provided political and financial support (e.g., guaranteed entrepreneurship loans) for employees engaged in innovation and entrepreneurship. Yet only those with a high level of human capital are able to start their own business, and their proportion among employees affected by reduced-capacity measures is small. Meanwhile, new startups can provide jobs for proportionately few people. Therefore, in general, innovative and entrepreneurial activity has a limited role in recruiting laid-off workers.

Thirdly, other supporting policies introduced by the government also have their problems when put into operation. Many are unsustainable, such as the special subsidy in the amount of RMB 100 billion earmarked for creating jobs for laid-offer workers, and the unemployment insurance used as subsidy to stabilize employment. The "internal retirement" policy, for example, allows employees to retire five years in advance. It reduces the burden on enterprises but increases the burden on endowment insurance.

Finally, male workers aged between 40 and 50 represent a large portion of those affected by capacity reduction. As a breadwinner in their household, they need more than temporary work, but a job in which they can create value. New approaches are needed to achieve this. The emergence of new forms of employment, represented by Didi Chuxing, has provided a new solution to the problem.

## 3    Data and Methods

In order to ensure the timeliness, accuracy, and reliability of our research, the research group has collected first-hand materials from Didi drivers in China's representative overcapacity provinces. The data of the program come from two sources—one is a nationwide sample survey of Didi Chuxing drivers, in particular the data collected through a special survey of Didi drivers in five pilot provinces. The other is Didi Chuxing platform itself, which provided us with its own data bank, which allowed us to cross-check data we collected from survey respondents on mileage, number of ride orders received, driving hours, cities in which they worked, among others.

The data given in the current research mainly come from: 1) the data of Didi drivers in Beijing, Shenzhen, Shanxi, Hebei, Heilongjiang, Jilin, and Liaoning, which was collected by the author when he conducted the programs respectively titled, "The Role of Didi Chuxing in Creating Employment Opportunities for Workers Laid-off Due to Overcapacity" and "The Impact of the Enforcement Regulations for Online Ride Hailing;" 2) questionnaires I distributed to Didi drivers in the aforementioned provinces/municipalities; and 3) an interview with Didi drivers, leasing companies in cooperation with the Didi platform, the Didi Chuxing headquarters, and local offices in the above-mentioned provinces/municipalities, which focuses on policy design and the driver management of the Didi platform, the contents and characteristics of jobs on the Didi platform, Didi operators' and drivers' comments about the job's characteristics, and their understanding of this new form of employment.

In terms of the research method, this chapter is a case study of the Didi Chuxing platform. Case studies are more suitable for "what to do" and "how to do,"[8] because such cases bring a comprehensive and holistic view of the phenomenon and its nature. This chapter starts with a look at the Didi platform, a representative of China's platform-based companies, and concludes with an in-depth analysis of the characteristics and mechanisms of platform-based companies more broadly.

This chapter focuses on the Didi Chuxing platform mainly because: 1) the Didi Chuxing platform has gathered 17.509 million drivers who have completed at least one transaction on the platform, and is the one of the largest employment platforms in both China and in the world;[9] 2) Uber, the counterpart of Didi Chuxing, is a worldwide representative of the sharing economy and the platform-based economy, and Didi Chuxing is quite similar to Uber in terms of employment characteristics and can thus represent platform-based companies more broadly; and 3) Didi Chuxing is a representative example of China's sharing economy, and can serve as the Chinese illustration of a global phenomenon.

## 4 Research Results

Based on a sample survey of Didi drivers nationwide, this chapter will describe the total number and distribution of jobs that the Didi platform has created for redundant workers, as well as the developmental trend of such employees on the Didi platform.

---

8  Walsham, G. "Interpretive Case Studies in IS Research: Nature and Method," *European Journal of Information Systems*, 2 (1995):74–81.

9  iResearch, "Research Report on the Service Market of China's Online Ride Hailing (2016)," 2016.

### 4.1 The Total Number of Flexible Jobs on the Didi Platform for Workers Affected by Capacity Reduction

The Didi platform has become an important area of reemployment for employees in overcapacity industries. According to the platform's own statistics and the survey conducted by the research group, from June 30, 2016 to June 30, 2017, the Didi Chuxing platform provided a total of 14.841 million jobs nationwide, including 9.172 million part-time jobs and 5.669 million full-time jobs. Over that same period, it provided 3.932 million jobs for employees in overcapacity industries, such as coal, steel, coal power, cement, chemical, and non-ferrous metals, including 2.746 million part-time jobs and 1.186 million full-time jobs. Specifically, it offered 0.352 million jobs for employees affected by capacity reduction in the coal and steel industries, 71 percent of which were part-time jobs and 29 percent full-time jobs. 285,000 people were unemployed until Didi provided them with the job opportunities, and all of them have become full-time Didi drivers, totally dependent on the Didi platform.

Throughout the country, a total of 1.788 million demobilized military personnel are engaged in online ride hailing on the Didi platform, including 505,400 full-time Didi drivers and 1.2829 million part-time Didi drivers. In the past year, over 50,000 newly demobilized military personnel joined the Didi platform as full-time Didi drivers. There are 159,000 ex-soldiers with more than 30 years of service, of which 48,500 are full-time Didi drivers.[10]

Of all the Didi drivers nationwide, 1.368 million (9.22 percent) are from zero-employment families (i.e., totally dependent on the Didi platform). The Didi platform has provided 34,000 (9.78 percent) job opportunities for workers affected by capacity reduction in the coal and steel industries that are from zero-employment families.

The Didi platform acts as an employment buffer in provinces with heavy capacity reduction tasks and heavy downward economic pressure. Figure 5.1 reveals the relationship between the provincial GDP growth rate and the proportion of otherwise unemployed Didi drivers on the provincial Didi platforms. As we can see in Figure 5.1, in provinces with slower economic growth, the proportion of otherwise unemployed Didi drivers are higher on the local Didi platforms, and vice versa.

Figure 5.2 shows the relationship between the growth rate of provincial per capita GDP and the proportion of Didi drivers from the coal and steel

---

10      Zhang Chenggang 张成刚, "Tuiyi junren zai didi pingtai jiuye qingkuan diaoyan baogao 退役军人在滴滴平台就业情况调研报告 [Research Report on the Employment of Demobilized Military Personnel on the Didi Platform]," WeChat Official Account "Renda renliziyuan 人大人力资源," July 31, 2017.

# THE ROLE OF PLATFORM-BASED COMPANIES

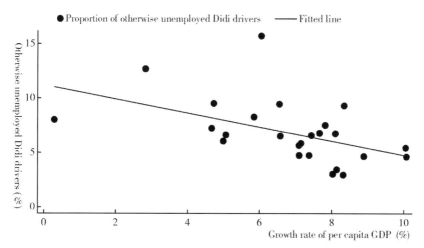

FIGURE 5.1   The relationship between provincial GDP growth rate and the proportion of otherwise unemployed Didi drivers

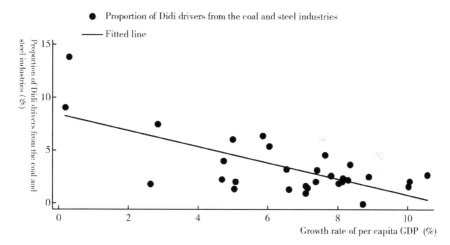

FIGURE 5.2   The relationship between the growth rate of provincial per capita GDP and the proportion of Didi drivers from the coal and steel industries

industries in 2016. We find a negative correlation between the two. That is, in provinces with a slowdown in 2016 per capita GDP growth, more drivers joined the Didi platform. Therefore, as we can see, the Didi platform plays the role of a reservoir for regional labor markets. When economic growth slows down or when a massive reduction in capacity affects employment, the Didi platform can absorb the surplus labor force by creating job opportunities, and thus pull the affected through their hardship.

## 4.2 *The Distribution of Workers Affected by Capacity Reduction Reemployed by the Didi Platform*

According to our statistics, in 224 cities among 31 provincial-level divisions, employees from overcapacity industries—such as steel, coal, and cement—have enrolled in the Didi platform. In 115 cities, employees from overcapacity industries—such as steel and coal—also serve as Didi Premier/Express drivers.

There is a positive correlation between the distribution of Didi drivers and regional economic development, population density, and the level of urbanization. The more economically developed provinces/municipalities, such as Beijing, Shanghai, Guangdong, Jiangsu, and Zhejiang, have a relatively high density of Didi drivers. Sichuan Province also has a relatively high density of Didi drivers—although it is in the western region, it still supports the development of Didi Chuxing.

As opposed to the overall distribution of Didi drivers, provinces/regions with a dense distribution of coal and steel workers are those with the most difficult task in terms of reducing coal and steel production in China, such as Shanxi, Hebei, Shandong, Inner Mongolia, and Xinjiang. This indicates that the Didi platform has become both a buffer for and reducer of pressure for the employment of workers affected by capacity reduction in these provinces/regions. While economic returns decline and some positions even disappear, to join the Didi platform and obtain a relatively stable income helps those employees affected by a reduction in industrial capacity overcome short-term hardships and is thus conducive to their connection with society and in preparation for reemployment.

According to the total number of registered drivers, we estimate the size of workers affected by capacity reduction in the overcapacity industries in five provinces (See Table 5.1).

TABLE 5.1    Number of workers affected by capacity reduction who found work on the Didi platform in pilot provinces (thousand)

| Province | All industries | Coal | Steel | Other overcapacity industries |
| --- | --- | --- | --- | --- |
| Shanxi | 532.7 | 53.3 | 20.3 | 53.9 |
| Hebei | 688.2 | 9.7 | 57.7 | 58.1 |
| Heilongjiang | 112.5 | 1.3 | 3.3 | 8.5 |
| Jilin | 124.2 | 1.2 | 4.3 | 13.1 |
| Liaoning | 234.4 | 2.8 | 25.6 | 17.8 |

## 4.3 Development of Didi Platform's Role in Creating Employment for Workers Affected by Capacity Reduction

With the development of the Didi platform and the declining earnings seen in the coal and steel industries, there has been a sharp rise in the number of workers who lost their jobs in overcapacity industries who then joined the Didi platform. Figure 5.3 shows the temporal distribution of registration on the Didi platform of all sample drivers and of workers affected by capacity reduction in the coal and steel industries in the five pilot provinces sampled. Figure 5.4 shows the temporal distribution of the first ride orders received on the Didi platform among all sample drivers and of workers affected by capacity reduction in the coal and steel industries in the five pilot provinces. As early as June 2014, some drivers had already joined the Didi platform. In January 2015, employees from the overcapacity industries of coal and steel started to join the

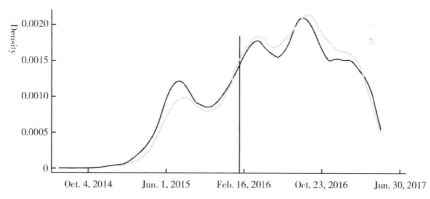

FIGURE 5.3    Temporal distribution of Didi registration

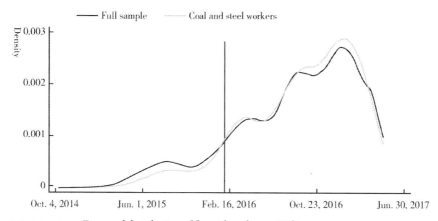

FIGURE 5.4    Temporal distribution of first ride orders on Didi

Didi platform, and since February 2015, they have been receiving ride orders on Didi. As we can see in Figures 5.3 and 5.4, since 2015 there had been significant increases in the number of registrations and first-time receipt of ride orders on the Didi platform by people formerly employed in the coal and steel industries.

As our samples were collected between January 2016 and April 2017, the registration and first ride orders appear to have fallen in April 2017, but that does not mean a decline in the total number of drivers registered and ride orders received on the Didi platform.

It is worth noting that before February 2016, both the number of former coal and steel industry workers who joined Didi and that of those who took their first ride order were lower than the aggregate numbers for all respondents. But the reverse was true afterward February 2016. In February 2016, the *Opinions of the State Council on Supporting the Coal Industry in Resolving Excess Production Capacity for the Purposes of Poverty Alleviation and Development* and the *Opinions of the State Council on Supporting the Steel Industry in Resolving Excess Production Capacity for the Purposes of Poverty Alleviation and Development* were published in succession, specifying the task of overcapacity reduction in the coal and steel industries and putting forward substantive requirements. In April 2016, the Ministry of Human Resources and Social Security, together with six other government authorities, issued the *Opinions on Employee Placement in the Process of Overcapacity Reduction and Poverty Alleviation in the Coal and Steel Industries*, which formally put forward measures for redundant worker placement in overcapacity industries. Since then, the number of registrations and initial ride orders of coal and steel workers on the Didi platform has surpassed those of all sample drivers. Obviously, the Didi platform has become an important choice for alleviating employment difficulties in the course of overcapacity reduction for the coal and steel industries.

In February 2016, when the State Council issued the *Opinions* on overcapacity reduction in the coal and steel industries, 9.3 percent of former workers in the coal and steel industries had already registered and started working on the Didi platform. In the process of overcapacity reduction, 75.7 percent of the redundant workers registered and joined the Didi platform in 2016. Even before the country's capacity reduction policy was introduced, the Didi platform was already a channel for certain former workers in the coal and steel industries to earn extra income. Since the State Council published the *Opinions* on overcapacity reduction, the Didi platform has become an even more important way out for those finding themselves in employment difficulties.

Based on our survey data, from January 2016 to the end of April 2017, the monthly growth rate of Didi drivers making an income reached 196 percent,

THE ROLE OF PLATFORM-BASED COMPANIES    115

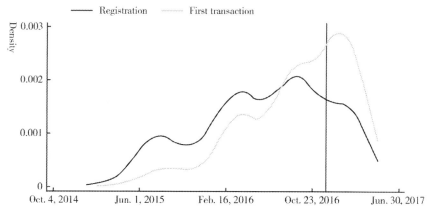

FIGURE 5.5    Temporal distribution of registration and first transactions on Didi by workers affected by capacity reduction in the steel and coal industries

and by the end of the first quarter of 2017, the number of Didi drivers making an income increased by 3.6 times compared with the same period over the previous year. In our samples from the coal and steel industries, the monthly growth rate of Didi drivers making an income was 177 percent. By the end of the first quarter of 2017, the number of active reduced capacity-affected drivers jumped by 4.58 times compared with the same period over the previous year.

The special program supporting the online ride hailing sector has provided strong incentives for redundant workers from the steel and coal industries to join the Didi platform. Figure 5.5 shows the difference in the temporal distribution of the number of registrations and first ride orders of the workers affected by capacity reduction in the steel and coal industries. As we can see in Figure 5.5, from 2015 to around July 2016, the registration density was higher than that of the number of first transactions on the Didi platform. This means that many workers affected by capacity reduction had, at that point, adopted a wait-and-see policy toward the Didi platform and, although they had joined the Didi platform, they had not yet started working on it. Yet starting in July 2016, the density of first transactions has been higher than that of registration. That is to say, registered employees started actually working on the Didi platform during this period. Particularly since the Ministry of Human Resources and Social Security and the Didi Chuxing Corporation commenced their special support program for the online ride hailing sector, the density of the number of first transactions has increased significantly. This reflects the effect of the policy in inspiring employees affected by reductions in capacity in the steel and coal industries to join the Didi platform. In particular, Shanxi Coking Coal Group featured prominently in this regard.

## 5    Conclusions

A significant hurdle to the placement of employees affected by capacity reductions is the sheer number of them. By comparison, corporations' ability to place these individuals within the organization is limited. If the market is flooded by a large number of these workers, social stability might be put in jeopardy. Therefore, we must find a way to create large number of jobs or earning opportunities in the short term.

The Didi platform provides a large number of jobs and does so quickly. Since it became operational, there has been an exponential rise in the number of drivers on the Didi platform, which represents fast and prolific job creation. Currently, 352,000 workers affected by capacity reduction in the coal and steel industries work on the Didi platform, accounting for 19.6 percent of 1.8 million, the estimated number of all redundant workers according to the Ministry of Human Resources and Social Security. An additional 3.579 million Didi drivers are from other overcapacity industries.

With the Chinese economy entering "the new normal," the acceleration of the country's industrial restructuring, transformation and upgrading, and the replacement of low-skilled laborers by machines and AI, many jobs in traditional manufacturing industries will disappear. In the short run, platform-based companies—represented by Didi—is able to absorb such laborers. As China's urbanization and upgrading of consumption services proceed, Didi Chuxing still has significant room for development. Meanwhile, with the extension of Didi's industrial chain, it also holds huge potential for the development of related businesses. Therefore, the Didi platform still represents an enormous potential pool of job opportunities, which is significant for workers affected by capacity reduction and who lost their jobs as a result of industrial transformation and upgrading.

In terms of the distribution of Didi drivers, their density reflects regional economic development. The more developed the economy, the higher permeability of the Didi platform.

At the same time, judging by the distribution and developmental trends of workers affected by capacity reduction on the platform, Didi has become a buffer and pressure reducer in provinces with the heaviest burdens of capacity reduction and economic pressure. In areas that face heavier job cuts to the coal and steel industries, the proportion of laid-off workers who end up joining the Didi platform tends also to be higher. And the rate at which these workers signed up with Didi picked up over time after February 2016, when full implementation of capacity reduction began. These trends in distribution and development indicate that the Didi platform can have some effect on the employment rate in the regional labor market in the short run.

In summation, the Didi platform has already provided a huge number of jobs for redundant workers and helped them attain relatively high incomes. Under the guidance of government policies, workers affected by capacity reduction are willing to work on the Didi platform for the long term on the condition of a low threshold of online ride hailing. The Didi platform—and the new forms of employment it represents—helps solve the dilemma of laborers' reemployment in the course of the country's supply-side reform and industrial upgrading.

## Acknowledgements

This chapter is the final installment of a work-in-progress report on the project titled *Mechanisms and Policy Assessment for New Forms of Employment to Support the Placement of Employees in Overcapacitated Sectors*. The project is co-funded by the National Social Science Fund of China and the scientific research fund of the Capital University of Business and Economics.

## Author Biography

Zhang Chenggang has a Ph.D. in economics and is an assistant professor at the School of Labor Economics, Capital University of Business and Economics. His academic interests include new forms of employment and labor market policy assessment.

## References

Didi Policy Research Institute, "Report on the Support of Online Ride Hailing for the Reemployment of Laid-off Workers in Key Reduced-Capacity Provinces," 2016.

Ding Shouhai 丁守海, "Zuidi gongzi guanzhi de jiuye xiaoying fenxi jianlun laodonghetongfa de jiaohu yingxiang 最低工资管制的就业效应分析—兼论〈劳动合同法〉的交互影响 [The Effect of Minimum-Wage Regulation on Employment and Its Interaction with the *Labor Contract Law*]," *Social Sciences in China* 1 (2010): 85–102, 223.

International Labor Organization (ILO), "The Future of Work Centenary Initiative," 2015.

iResearch, "Research Report on the Service Market of China's Online Ride Hailing (2016)," 2016.

Li Xiaoman 李晓曼, "Huajie channengguosheng zhong de shouyingxiang zhigong guimo xianzhuang yu anzhi duice 化解产能过剩中的受影响职工：规模、现状与安置对策 [Workers Affected by Capacity Reduction: Number, Condition, and Placement Measures]," *Human Resource Development of China* 6 (2017): 18–24.

State Information Center (SIC) Research Center of Sharing Economy and The Internet Society of China (ISC) Sharing Economy Working Committee, *Report on the Development of China's Sharing Economy* (2017).

Tang Kuang, Li Yanjun, and Xu Jingyun 唐镔、李彦君、徐景昀, "Gongxiang jingji qiye yonggong guanli yu laodonghetongfa zhidu chuanxin 共享经济企业用工管理与《劳动合同法》制度创新 [Employment Management of Sharing Economy Enterprises and the Institutional Innovation of the Labor Contract Law]," China Labor 14 (2016): 41–52.

Walsham, G. "Interpretive Case Studies in IS Research: Nature and Method," *European Journal of Information Systems*, 2 (1995):74–81.

Zhang Chenggang 张成刚, "Jiuye fazhan de weilai qushi xin jiuye xingyai de gainian ji yingxiang fenxin 就业发展的未来趋势，新就业形态的概念及影响分析 [The Future Trend of Employment Development: The Concept and Influence of New Forms of Employment]," Human Resource Development of China 19 (2016): 86–91.

Zhang Chenggang 张成刚, "Tuiyi junren zai didi pingtai jiuye qingkuan diaoyan baogao 退役军人在滴滴平台就业情况调研报告 [Research Report on the Employment of Demobilized Military Personnel on the Didi Platform]," WeChat Official Account "Renda renliziyuan 人大人力资源," July 31, 2017.

CHAPTER 6

# Policy Support System for Innovative Industries

*Cai Yifei and Wang Boya*

## 1 China's Policy Support System for Innovative Industries: Current Condition and Problems

Promoting the development of innovative industries is an inevitable choice that China will make to catch up with and surpass developed countries. Yet in a developing country with an incomplete market and institutional environment, innovative industries can hardly take root and grow without powerful policy support, and will thus take a longer time to catch up with developed countries. Therefore, since the implementation of its Torch Program in 1988, China has endeavored to establish a policy support system for the development of innovative industries. Only when we understand the policy support system for innovative industries can we discover the problems that remain and make improvements, so as to provide more fertile soil for the growth of innovative industries.

### 1.1 Basic Information about China's Policy Support System for Innovative Industries

We review China's policy support system for three major innovative industries, taking three primary three perspectives on the matter: policy strategies—including industrial development strategies and basic plans formulated by the central government, general laws and regulations—which are not specially formulated for a particular industry but contain applicable policies, and special policies—policy documents introduced by the state to boost the development of an industry. Table 6.1 shows the results.

#### 1.1.1 High-Tech Industries
China's high-tech industrial policies started in the 1990s. Over the course of more than 30 years of development, a policy system has come into being which consists of two dimensions (the central and local dimensions) as well as two types of principal parts (enterprises and development zones). In this policy system, national hi-tech industrial development zones form the core.

The state formulates general policies, including tax preferences for high-tech enterprises and master plans for development zones. Local governments and development zone governments implement the general policies introduced by the state and formulate local policies oriented toward the agglomeration of industrial clusters and a business climate conducive to industrial development.

Enterprise-level policies mainly refer to preferential tax policies for high-tech enterprises. The correct identification of high-tech enterprises is the basis for the implementation of various preferential policies. In 2008, China introduced the *Administrative Measures for the Determination of High- and New-Technology Enterprises* and revised it in 2016, putting forward standards outlining high- and new-technology enterprises. Meanwhile, the *Law of the People's Republic of China on the Administration of Tax Collection, Detailed Rules for the Implementation of the Law of the People's Republic of China on the Administration of Tax Collection, Administrative Measures for the Determination of High- and New-Technology Enterprises*, and the *Enterprise Income Tax Law* have all stipulated preferential tax policies for high-tech enterprises. In terms of enterprise income tax, high- and new-technology enterprises pay a tax rate of 15 percent, ten percentage points lower than ordinary enterprises. In terms of import and export taxes, imported equipment used for the production of those products listed on the *National New Technology Product Catalogue* are exempted from tariff and import value-added taxes. For enterprises' importation of apparatuses and equipment directly used in scientific research, experiment, and teaching, the import value-added tax is exempted. For fixed assets invested by enterprises, if it is indeed necessary for accelerated depreciation due to technological progress, they may shorten the depreciation period or simply accelerate the depreciation.

Development zones are spatial carriers for the clustered development of high and new technology industries. They are platforms that integrate various high-tech elements, such as knowledge, information, capital, management, and talents. The primary function of development zone policies is to optimize the climate for industrial and corporate development, implement the state's industrial policies, and formulate supportive policies according to the *Interim Measures for the Administration of National High-Tech Industrial Development Zones*. Local governments have a relatively broad degree of freedom in decision-making as it relates to development zones, and their support for development zones varies according to their financial strength and the weight they give to development zones. Generally speaking, the stronger their financial standing and the more weight they give to development zones, the greater their support for development zones tends to be. Regional development zone policies mainly include the provision of various industrial incubators, the establishment of various financing platforms and industrial development guidance funds, preferential policies on land development, the development of high- and new-technology services, and the establishment of supportive service systems for industrial development, among others.

### 1.1.2 Strategic Emerging Industries

Compared with the country's high-tech industries, China's strategic emerging industries have not yet developed into a mature system, and consequently any supportive industrial policies are scattered across special policy documents in the form of special funds for industrial development and industrial tax preferences. A prominent problem in industrial policy-making for strategic emerging industries is that the classification of industries is not consistent with the standard industry catalogue, creating difficulties in identifying the policy object. Moreover, such classifications overlap with those of high-tech industries in terms of the policy object. For example, over 70 percent of these types of sectors overlap in the *Catalogue of Key High-Tech Areas Supported by the State* and in the *Directory of Key Products and Services for Strategic Emerging Industries*. As a result, the tax preferences for strategic emerging industries are usually based on existing industrial policies. For example, the *Circular of the State Council on Issuing Policies to Further Encourage the Development of Software and Integrated Circuit Industries* stipulates preferential value-added tax and corporate income tax in software and integrated circuit industries. *The Enterprise Income Tax Law* and its implementation rules stipulate that enterprises are entitled to a 10 percent tax credit for their investment in special equipment aimed at environmental protection, along with energy- and water-saving equipment. Another example, the *Notice on Adjusting the Catalogue and Regulations of Import Tax Policy for Major Technological Equipment* stipulates relevant tax preferences for "integrated resource utilization," "energy saving and emission cutting," "technologically advanced service enterprises," and "the import of major technological equipment."

Although there is no special fiscal or tax policy for strategic emerging industries, they enjoy a new policy window—strategic emerging industries have a natural combination of advantages with capital. As the capital market becomes increasingly developed in China, there are abundant financial tools already ready for their use. To this end, the Ministry of Finance and the National Development and Reform Commission issued the *Interim Measures for the Management of Venture Capital Funds with Shares in Venture Capital Plans of Emerging Industries*. Under the guidance of such documents, the state's special financial funds raise more money for strategic emerging industries using capital market instruments. This is a unique advantage of strategic emerging industries.

### 1.1.3 Intellectual Property-Intensive Industries

China has just recently begun to develop its intellectual property-intensive industries, and as such there are relatively few supportive industrial policies in place at present, and those that do exist mainly take the form of guiding opinions on the industrial development of national strategies. For example, the *Opinions of the State Council on Accelerating the Construction of a Powerful Intellectual Property Country Under the New Situation* and the *Circular of the State Council on the Issuance of the National Strategic Emerging Industries Development Plan for the 13th Five-Year Plan Period* pay special attention to the construction of an intellectual property system and the cultivation of an intellectual property environment, as well as introduce supportive measures concerning investment, financing, the reformation of government administration, etc. Such institutional measures actually reduce the transaction costs for the development of intellectual property-intensive industries and, in an indirect way, boost the development of such industries. To meet the challenges raised by ongoing changes in the country's domestic and international economic environment, China has begun to deploy intellectual property-intensive industries. In 2012, the *Measures for the Assessment and Management of National Intellectual Property Pilot Demonstration Parks* was formulated, and by January 2017, approximately 100 such parks had been established. These pilot parks are designed to be the major carriers of industrial policies

TABLE 6.1 Major supportive documents for the development of innovative industries

| Industries | Strategic policy documents | Special policies | General laws and regulations |
|---|---|---|---|
| High-tech industries | China Torch Program | Decision on Strengthening Technological Innovation, Developing High Technology, and Realizing Industrialization | Law of the People's Republic of China on the Progress of Science and Technology |
| | Outline of Development Planning for National High-Tech Industrial Development Zones | | |
| | | Interim Measures for the Administration of National High-Tech Industrial Development Zones | Enterprise Income Tax Law Implementation Rules of the Enterprise Income |
| | | Interim Provisions on Certain Policies Concerning National High- and New-Technology Industrial Development Zones | Tax Law |
| | | | Government Purchase Law |

POLICY SUPPORT SYSTEM FOR INNOVATIVE INDUSTRIES 123

TABLE 6.1 Major supportive documents for the development of innovative (*cont.*)

| Industries | Strategic policy documents | Special policies | General laws and regulations |
|---|---|---|---|
| Strategic emerging industries | The Decision of the State Council on Accelerating the Fostering and Development of Strategic Emerging Industries<br><br>The 13th Five-Year Plan for the Development of China's Strategic Emerging Industries | Interim Measures for the Management of Venture Capital Fund with Shares in Venture Capital Plans of Emerging Industries<br><br>Interim Measures for the Management of Special Funds for the Development of Strategic Emerging Industries<br><br>Guidelines for Special Bond Issuance in Strategic Emerging Industries<br><br>Notice on Enterprise Income Tax Policy to Further Encourage the Development of the Software and Integrated Circuit Industries<br><br>Notice on the Business Tax and Value-Added Tax Policies to Support the Development of the Animation Industry | Law of the People's Republic of China on the Promotion of Small and Medium-Sized Enterprises<br><br>Provisional Regulations on Value-Added Tax<br><br>Decision on Strengthening Technological Innovation, Developing High Technology and Realizing Industrialization<br><br>Notice on Tax Policies for Major Special Imports of Science and Technology<br><br>Patent Law<br><br>Trademark Law<br><br>Copyright Law |

TABLE 6.1    Major supportive documents for the development of innovative *(cont.)*

| Industries | Strategic policy documents | Special policies | General laws and regulations |
| --- | --- | --- | --- |
| Intellectual-property-intensive industries | Opinions of the State Council on Accelerating the Construction of a Powerful Intellectual Property Country Under the New Situation; <br><br> Outline of the National Intellectual Property Strategy | Administrative Measures for the Application of Foreign Patent Funds; <br><br> Management Measures for National Intellectual Property Pilot Demonstration Parks | |

SOURCE: SORTED BY THE AUTHOR.

for intellectual property-intensive industries. In 2016, the National Intellectual Property Administration published the *Patent-Intensive Industry Catalogue 2016*, specifying the object of industrial policies. In the future, it will set more rules for a wider range of intellectual property-intensive industries, including the protection of copyright and brands.

### 1.2    *Major Problems with the Policies Supporting Innovative Industries*

The existing industrial policies are not only guides and future plans, but also contain supportive measures for investment, financing, and the reformation of government administration. With so many objectives and plans, however, there are large areas of overlap among industrial policies at the operational level, and there are gaps between policy design and their actual operation. We have identified four main problems with China's supportive policies for innovative industries.

First of all, China's policy support system for innovative industries is not complete. The aforementioned three innovative industries are different in their characteristics and their mission within the innovative economy, yet they are all an indispensable part of the innovative economy. The strategic emerging industries are vague in their policy objects and relatively decentralized in terms of policy. They overlap with high-tech industries in their supporting policies. The intellectual property-intensive industries are an important link to

China's innovative industrial system, but there is still no plan or policy specially made for them. Even though there are strategic outlines and guiding opinions for their development, a special policy for the industrialization of intellectual property is still lacking.

Secondly, the policy support being offered is not strong enough. In recent years, China has made significant progress in research and development, but is still far behind developed countries. In 2015, China's research and development expenses accounted for 2.1 percent of its GDP, yet this figure is eclipsed by the average of 3 percent or 4 percent set aside for R&D by developed countries. As the funds provided by the government cannot meet the existing need for the transformation of scientific and technological achievements, some fruits have withered on the vine even though they are well worth further development and would likely bring considerable market returns. In terms of the industrialization of intellectual property, China has not yet established a long-term mechanism for any increase in financial support, and it has invested relatively little in patent examination, public services for intellectual property, and research and planning on intellectual property.

Thirdly, the structure of financial input as it stands is unreasonable. During the research and development stage, the input of funds is abundant, but funds are much less forthcoming during the pilot testing and industrialization stages, causing many excellent scientific and technological achievements to fail to realize their full economic values. Abuse of preferential policies and an absence of policy go hand-in-hand. The existing supportive policies only target certain industries, but give little consideration to the innovativeness of enterprises. For enterprises listed in the catalogue of high- and new-technology industries, a simple procedure entitles them to large tax preferences, while there are no such tax incentives for knowledge-intensive enterprises and products. What's more, enterprises within the high-tech zones almost invariably enjoy tax preferences no matter whether they themselves are high-tech enterprises or not. There is no withdrawal and adjustment mechanism for these preferential policies. For example, some enterprises still enjoy tax preferences even though they are technologically backward, and consequently, they will lose the incentive for further innovation.

Finally, there is no effective coordination between the existing policies, resulting in separate and disorderly implementation. For strategic emerging industries, the major focus is on supporting programs and utilizing special financial programs, while for high-tech industries, supportive industrial policies are limited to the development zones. Both lack a strategic layout or any guidance for intellectual property. On the other hand, although knowledge-intensive industries pay adequate attention to intellectual property policies, the implementation of such policies has been ineffective. The guiding and regulatory policies for innovative industries are poorly coordinated with local industrial planning and regional innovative construction, an issue that intensifies regional competition for research, development, and talent. There is no effective connection between policies, the existing supportive policies are inadequate and incomplete, and the superimposed effect of multiple policies is insignificant. For example, both strategic emerging industries and knowledge-intensive industries have formulated their own individual talent policies, but such policies are torn between talent cultivation and the demands imposed by innovative industries. Under the current system, it is difficult to effectively implement talent incentivization policies, and therefore it is difficult to form a system covering the cultivation of talent, talents' entry into innovative positions, and market support for the cultivation of further talent.

## 2       The Adjustment Orientation of China's Supportive Policies for Innovative Industries

### 2.1     *Improve Top-Level Design for the Policy Support System*

A most critical problem in the development of China's innovative industries is the lack of systematic and normative policies. Not only do these systems exhibit overlap or the repetition of certain policies, but they also suffer from the absence of policies covering certain important aspects. This is mainly because the policies for innovative industries are formulated by different authorities. Specifically, the formulation of supportive policies for high-tech industries is dominated by the Ministry of Science and Technology; that of strategic emerging industries by the National Development and Reform Commission; and that of intellectual property-intensive industries by the National Intellectual Property Administration. Such industrial policies have a wide range of coverage but blurred boundaries. For example, the three industries listed previously are basically the same in terms of tax preferences, investment subsidies, and soft loans, but they all have the problem of an absence of policy dealing with government purchases, information services, standard setting, etc. In order to solve both the repetition of and absence of policies, it is necessary to first improve the legal system governing these innovative industries, and to normalize and comprehensively protect innovative achievements and their industrialization from an economic, scientific and technological, educational, and administrative perspective. We recommend establishing a coordinating organization for innovative industrial policies, to organize a cross-ministerial joint conference for innovative industries, and to set up a national advisory committee for the further development of innovative industries. We also recommend an examination and assessment of the formulation of relevant policies and a normalization of the boundaries of restrictive policies based on industrial characteristics.

### 2.2    *Establish a Pluralistic Governance System for Innovative Industries*

Society is a complex yet open, evolutionary network system of coupling effects and adaptations. Industrial governance under such a complex social environment is a complicated system project. With the arrival of globalization and the internet era—as well as the ongoing changes to the governing philosophy of the state and society—industrial governance has shifted from one of linear administration dominated by the government to joint governance and collaborative governance. Traditional industrial policies give more consideration to the role of public policies in industrial development, and have not taken into account interactive mechanisms, resulting either in over-interference in the market mechanism or the absence of supportive policies urgently needed by enterprises. In order to fundamentally solve this problem, it is necessary to establish an industrial governance system and formulate a policy system that is in line with multilateral interests under the framework of industrial governance.

The ideal framework for industrial governance is characterized by full participation, good interaction, and efficient coordination. It incorporates the legal, institutional, social, and economic conditions of industrial governance into the variable known as "situational structure," thus establishing a governance network in which multiple entities participate, such as the government, industrial organizations, enterprises, research institutes, NGOs, citizens, etc. It breaks through the dual governance model dominated by the market and the government, makes up for market and government failures in industrial governance, establishes a multi-layered industrial support system and resource allocation system, and, by establishing an industrial operation mechanism, focuses on solving the cross-ministerial problems endemic to industrial governance. The establishment of an industrial governance framework includes a cross-ministerial joint conference for the development of innovative industries, a policy advisory committee, and a coordinating organization for the coordinated development of innovative industries. Meanwhile, it is necessary to formulate guiding opinions on the development of innovative industries and normalize the planning and policy systems of the three innovative industries, so as to lay an institutional foundation for the establishment of an industrial governance system. What's more, it is also necessary to improve the existing support system for the industrialization of intellectual property, and to boost the establishment of innovative industry associations and technical alliances at the state and local levels and in the country's development zones. We propose boosting the development of innovative services, cultivating a number of innovative service institutions and leading enterprises, and shaping clusters of innovative services. We also propose the establishment and improvement of a system of intellectual property navigation and legal assistance, so as to lower the operational costs of innovative enterprises.

## 2.3 *Improve the Precision and Differentiation of Industrial Policies*

The policies supporting innovative industries must change from a broad flood of support to more precise targeting. The objects of industrial policies include sectors and enterprises. Sectoral policies are public policies made for a group of enterprises that are similar in terms of their products and technological characteristics, while their goal is to cultivate a favorable environment for the development of such enterprises. Corporate policies, on the other hand, refer to preferential policies directly targeting enterprises. Be they sectoral or corporate policies, the ultimate effect of policies should be on enterprises.

We must combine relaxation and regulation, distinguish regional and industrial differences, inspire enthusiasm for innovation and creation, and actively prevent potential risks. For strategic industries with strong correlation but weak comparative advantages, we may cultivate their strengths and further improve them using fiscal, financial, and industrial policies. For those emerging industries with bright prospects and controllable risks, we must give preferential treatment to those policies that favor them. For industries with neither comparative advantages nor bright prospects, we must strengthen our systems of monitoring and analysis in order to select the superior and eliminate the inferior. For those traditional industries that turn a profit in the name of innovation (or what is known in Chinese as "old wine in a new bottle"), we must exclude them from the list of demonstration parks or model enterprises.

We must differentiate the design of sectoral policies from corporate policies. The country's sectoral policies are designed to cultivate an environment predicated on and leading to development and reduce the overall transaction costs of a sector/industry; they must create a stage characterized by fair competition among enterprises within the same industry while also bringing into play the market mechanism necessary for higher overall efficiency and competitiveness. After all, to boost industrial development is to improve the technological level and capacity for innovation of enterprises. Therefore, industrial policies must be grounded on the scientific and accurate identification of innovative enterprises. The basis for the accurate support of corporate policies is the establishment of an accurate statistical database. We must integrate corporate information in the hands of related departments (e.g., the statistical system, technological parks, etc.) and establish a corporate database. Meanwhile, we must create a set of standards and select eligible enterprises from among many options.

# Index

active drivers 69
administrative regulations and rules 54
aging problem 24
AI (Artificial Intelligence) 39–40, 54, 116
annual employment growth 1–2, 11
application platforms 54
asset-liability ratio 79
average individual monthly income 74
average monthly income 98
average number of working hours 51

big data 39, 42, 53, 64
big data analysis 31, 62

capital 8, 13, 24, 34, 36, 42, 51, 61, 63, 108, 120–121
capital market 121
China's employment 11, 18, 26, 34, 38, 44–45
China's employment rate 22–23
China's GDP 1–2, 4–6, 12, 19, 26–27
China's labor market 30, 35, 47, 52
China's new economic sectors 3, 6, 9, 11, 19, 21, 29
China's new economy 1, 3–6, 10, 12, 14, 19, 44
China's new employment 22, 31–32
China's overall employment 2, 9–11, 19, 23, 26
China's sharing economy 67–68, 106, 109
classification of industries 121
collaborative governance 127
collective-owned enterprises 56
commercial endowment insurance 84
commercial insurance 84, 93
commercial medical insurance 84, 93
conventional models of business 34
copyright 122
corporate policies 128–129

data economy 34
data technology 31, 39–42, 62
demand side 18, 20, 106
density of Didi drivers 112
development zones 21, 119–120, 125, 128
Didi Chuxing 29, 69, 106, 108–109, 112, 115–116

Didi Chuxing platform 9, 106, 108–110
Didi drivers 53, 68–69, 83, 90–93, 95, 97–98, 101–102, 106, 108–110, 112, 114–116
digital economy 29–30, 34, 36, 37, 39
digital modes of marketing 31
digital technology 22–23, 29–30, 34–35, 37–39, 103
direct contribution 3, 9–10
division of labor 1, 53
division of labor and trade 19
driving experience 69, 93
dual governance model 127

economically active population 26
emerging industries 2–3, 5, 7–8, 10, 12, 19–21, 30, 38, 121–122, 124–126, 128
employee mobility 58, 63
employers 41, 48, 55–64, 83
employment 2, 9–10, 14, 17–41, 44–53, 57–64, 67, 69, 71, 73, 79–80, 83, 87, 100–102, 105–106, 108–112, 114
employment absorption 26, 46
employment growth 1–2, 8–9, 11, 19, 22–23, 26, 31
employment integration 15–18
employment models 41–42, 105
employment rate 22–25, 116
employment structure 34, 44–46, 52
endowment insurance 59, 84, 92–93, 108
external compulsory constraints 62

family planning 24
first-tier cities 98
fixed working hours 49, 62
fixed workplaces 52, 62
flexible employees 57, 60
flexible employment 18, 35–36, 47, 51–52, 57, 59, 64
flexible work schedules 48
flexible working time 49
foreign-funded enterprises 56, 80
formal employment 52, 57, 60
formal labor relations 59, 63
freelancers 36, 41–42, 47, 53, 61, 80, 87

132 INDEX

full-time Didi drivers   90–93, 95, 98, 101, 110
full-time drivers   68, 87, 93, 95, 97–98
full-time online ride-hailing drivers   72 n. 6,
    86
full-time ride share drivers   70, 77, 86–87,
    101–102

grassroots trade unions   56

high- and new-technology enterprises   120
high-tech enterprises   47, 120, 125
high-tech industries   2, 5–6, 21, 45, 119, 121,
    124–126
high-tech zones   125
household income-expenditure ratio   79
Housing Provident Fund   83–84
human capital   8, 24, 35, 43, 51, 61, 63, 108

income elasticity of employment   25
individual employment   22, 32
industrial classification   37
industrial governance   127
industrial governance system   127
industrial policies   119–122, 124–128
industrial policy making   121
industrial structure   18, 20, 26, 44–45, 54
industrial technology   62
industrial trade unions   64
informal employees   53
informal employment   48, 52, 59–60, 63–64,
    105
informal labor relations   63
information technology   2, 7, 12, 30–31, 34,
    41, 53, 62, 64
innovation-driven development strategy
    46, 67
innovative industries   119, 124, 126–128
innovative services   53, 128
institutional and structural barriers   63
intellectual property policies   125
intellectual property system   122
intellectual property-intensive industries   2,
    122, 124, 126
inter-disciplinary talents   35, 40
internal compulsory constraints   62
Internet of Things   30, 39
internet platforms   29, 53
internet-based economy   30

job classification   38
job markets   30
job opportunities   8–9, 18, 32, 34, 39–40, 47,
    51, 59, 67, 80, 91, 101, 106, 110–111, 116
joint governance   127

knowledge-intensive enterprises   125

labor contracts   55, 57–59, 64
labor dispute settlement mechanisms   55
labor laws   54–55, 59, 102
labor regulations   63
labor market   30, 34–35, 37–39, 41–42, 47,
    52, 55, 58, 63, 101–102, 106, 111, 116
labor participation rate   23
labor productivity   13–14, 26
labor protection   59
labor relations   29, 36, 44–45, 54–60, 63–64,
    68, 103
labor security   21, 55, 58, 68
labor unions   56–57, 60, 64
labor-intensive   17, 46
labor-market reforms   32
laborers' rights and interests   55–60
laborers' working hours   49–51
laid-off workers   47, 106, 108, 116
legal limits on working hours   50
linear administration   127

market economy   55
market-based labor regulations   55, 63
market demand   30, 39, 48
mass entrepreneurship and innovation   12,
    67
medical insurance   59, 83–84, 92–93
middle-income trap   25, 38
migrant workers   47, 56–57
mismatch between supply and demand   13
modes of employment   57, 101
monthly driving hours   97
monthly household expenditures   75
monthly household income   75
multi-layered support system   127

new economic sectors   1–6, 8–9, 11–16,
    18–21, 29
new economy   1–6, 8–20, 22, 29–30, 36,
    39–41, 44–49, 51–53, 57–60, 62–64, 106

INDEX

new employment   19–20, 22, 29, 31–32, 35, 37, 40, 44, 46–47, 57–60, 62–64
new first-tier cities   100
new forms of employment   18, 21, 23, 46, 48–49, 51–52, 57, 59–60, 62–64, 105, 108, 117
new models of business   29, 44–46, 60, 62, 67, 105
new normal   44, 116
new work methods   62
new-economic development   1–2, 6, 8
new-economic sectors   1–6, 8–9, 11–12, 14, 16, 18
new-economic-boosted sectors   13
new-economy-boosted employment   9–10
new-economy-boosted sectors   2–3, 5, 9, 11
new-employment laborer's   59, 62–64
new-model economy   5–6
new-model sector(s)   1, 6, 10–11, 13–14, 19
new-technology economy   5, 45
new-technology sector(s)   6, 10–11, 13
non-public enterprises   55–56

online finance   53
online rideshare drivers   101–102
online ridesharing   79, 98, 100–101
output of labor   28
overall employment   1–2, 9–11, 15, 18–19, 23, 26, 40, 44, 46, 102
overall productivity   13
overcapacity industries   9, 13, 106, 110, 112–114, 116
overcapacity reduction   114

part-time Didi drivers   83, 95, 98, 101, 110
part-time drivers   29, 80–81, 83–84, 86, 95, 97–98
patent examination   125
platform economy   35
platform enterprises   3, 6, 37, 39, 49, 68
platform-based companies   23, 106, 109
platform-based freelancers   36
platform-based models of employment   105
policy support   6, 119, 125
policy support system   119, 124
preferential policies   120–121, 125, 128
private enterprises   56, 62, 87–88
proportion in GDP   5

protection of laborers' rights and interests   55–60, 63–64

redundant worker placement   114
reemployment   106, 110, 112, 117
research and development expenses   125
ride orders   69, 95, 108, 113–114–115
ride-hailing drivers   71, 87
   online ride hailing   68, 70–71, 79, 90–91, 93, 95, 98, 101, 107, 110, 115, 117
   online ride-hailing drivers   68–69, 72–75, 77–80, 86, 100
   online ride-hailing income   79
   online ride-hailing market   100–101
   part-time ride-hailing drivers   72

secondary industry   26–27, 50
sectoral policies   128
service industry   46
sharing economy   18, 21, 29, 34, 36–37, 46, 49, 57–57, 59, 67–68, 72, 79–80, 86, 100–102, 107, 109
sharing economy platforms   46, 58, 106, 109
sharing platforms   29–30, 53
social dependency ratio   79
social insurance   36, 53, 57, 59
social security   106, 114–116
social security policy   102
social security system   35–36, 39, 41–42, 102
standard number of working hours   49–50
state-owned enterprises   56, 80
strategic emerging industries   2–3, 5, 7–8, 10, 12, 21, 121, 124–126
structural unemployment   20, 40
subsidy   108
supply side   13, 18, 106
supply-side reform   20, 44, 67, 117
supportive industrial policies   121–122, 125
supportive measures   122–124

task-oriented work relations   58
tax policies   120
tertiary industry   22–23, 26–28, 31, 46, 51, 70, 106
the sharing economy   18, 21, 29, 36–37, 46, 49, 57–59, 67–68, 72, 79–80, 86, 100–102, 106, 109
top-level design   126

trade unions   56, 64, 103
traditional forms of employment   41, 58, 105
transformation and upgrading   12–14, 18, 22, 40, 46, 107, 116

unemployment insurance   83, 108

value added   1–6, 12, 16–17, 26, 37, 120–121
vehicle conditions   95

ways of working   52
withdrawal and adjustment mechanism   125
work behavior   95

work methods   62
workers affected by capacity reduction   108, 110, 112–113, 115–117
working conditions   44, 48, 52, 68, 72
working efficiency   48, 51, 61
working hours   29–30, 48–51, 60–62, 83, 87, 90, 105
working modes   29, 48
working-age population   22, 24, 25
workplaces   51–52, 60, 62

zero-employment families   110

Printed in the United States
By Bookmasters